David A. Wolfe
Christine Wekerle
Robert Gough
Deborah Reitzel-Jaffe
Carolyn Grasley
Anna-Lee Pittman
Lorraine Lefebvre
Jennifer Stumpf

The Youth Relationships Manual

A Group Approach
With Adolescents
for the Prevention
of Woman Abuse
and the
Promotion of
Healthy
Relationships

SAGE Publications
International Educational and Professional Publisher
Thousand Oaks London New Delhi

For information address:

SAGE Publications, Inc.
2455 Teller Road
Thousand Oaks, California 91320
E-mail: order@sagepub.com

SAGE Publications Ltd.
6 Bonhill Street
London EC2A 4PU
United Kingdom

SAGE Publications India Pvt. Ltd.
M-32 Market
Greater Kailash I
New Delhi 110 048 India

Printed in the United States of America

Library of Congress Cataloging-in-Publication Data

Wolfe, David A.
    The youth relationships manual: A group approach with adolescents for the prevention of woman abuse and the promotion of healthy relationships / authors, David A. Wolfe . . . [et al.].
        p.   cm.
    Includes bibliographical references.
    ISBN 0-7619-0194-9 (pbk.: acid-free paper)
    1. Youth Relationships Project (London, Ont.).   2. Social work with teenagers—Canada—Case studies.   3. Social work with youth—Canada—Case studies.   4. Interpersonal relations in adolescence—Study and teaching—Canada—Case studies.   5. Dating violence—Canada—Prevention—Case studies.   6. Women—Abuse of—Canada—Prevention—Case studies.   I. Title.
    HV1441.C3W65   1996
    362.8—dc20   95-50179

This book is printed on acid-free paper.

96 97 98 99 00 01 10 9 8 7 6 5 4 3 2 1

Sage Production Editor: Tricia K. Bennett
Sage Typesetter: Andrea D. Swanson

Contents

Preface

*With violence in schools, racism, AIDS, peer pressure to
take drugs and alcohol, and the poor future job market,
our concerns need to be dealt with now, not later.
(Marla Brown, "Youth Voice Needs Outlet,"
London Free Press, April 21, 1994)*

Youth have problems, not solutions. This is the message from
Marla Brown, the student quoted above, and a theme we hear from
many youth. There is a sense of urgency to the youth of today—a
demand and plea—for "voice and choice." Fundamentally, the
present-day struggle of youth is like the struggle of any marginal-
ized group in our society. This is a struggle about power.

> Power and personal agency are important expressions of
> many other factors: individuality, freedom, responsibility
> and viability. (Mahoney, 1991, p. 183)

Power and power processes (i.e., who has the "final say" in
decisions, who has access to resources) are "driving forces" in so
many areas of our lives: in education; in the workplace; in our
communities, neighborhoods, and homes; and in our relationships. Previous and present movements, such as women's rights,
human rights, peace, freedom, ecology, and health, testify to the
capacity of humans for action, commitment, and creativity in
effecting positive change through positive use of power assertion.
However, power processes can go awry, chiefly when there are
static and significant imbalances in power, dichotomizing persons,
groups, and settings into the advantaged and disadvantaged, the
"haves" and the "have nots," and the one-up and one-down power
structure.

The youth of today find themselves among the relatively
powerless; they are on the receiving end of so many forms of
discrimination, adding adultism to the long list: racism, heterosex-
ism, ableism, sexism, and classism. Furthermore, youth are confronted with no shortage of experts: people who identify the
problems of youth, the "what" of change—teen violence, teen

pregnancy, teen illiteracy, teen unemployment—but who offer very little to assist in the "how" or ways of change and the "why" or motivation for change and, importantly, how to remain resilient in the face of the "why not" or "why bother" to change.

The Youth Relationships Project (YRP) is aiming to address relationships as our main targets for change. We address the various contexts in which these relationships appear in society, family, and social contexts as well as the attitudinal, cognitive, and behavioral skills aspects of relationships. Relationships are inevitable parts of our lives, and when power imbalances define these, we are more likely to experience abuse in relationships: child abuse and neglect, peer aggression and rejection, partner violence, and victimization and sexual assault.

Researchers and clinicians have come to understand that violence is a cycle that is likely to continue across generations unless something or someone intervenes. The prevention of violence in relationships (abuse, neglect, and negative interaction) and the promotion of health in relationships (nurturance, protection, and positive interaction) are valuable for all individuals, because there is no "ceiling" or upper limit to relationship skills and success. The prevention of relationship violence and power abuses is also highly salient for vulnerable youth—those individuals whose sense of self, stability, and lovability has become a painful struggle that can last a lifetime—again, if something is not done about it. The Youth Relationships Project is something that can be done.

The purpose of this YRP manual and its companion volume, *Alternatives to Violence: Empowering Youth to Promote Healthy Relationships* (Wolfe, Wekerle, & Scott, in press), is to assist adults in empowering youth to end violence in relationships (their own and that of their peers) through education, skill development, and social competence. The program material takes teens through a process of learning about the issue and about themselves and then expands their efforts to effect change within their peer groups, the teen culture, and the broader community. It reflects an incremental strategy aimed at self-awareness and social change (self, peers, school environment, social institutions, culture). Personal learning and motivation is reinforced by working toward social change.

Although this process is broken out into sections in the manual, as the work evolves it is important to provide skill development as early as possible and to rehearse these skills throughout the group when "natural" opportunities arise. In addition, most antiviolence educational materials available show *what the problem is* and thus teach *what not to do;* therefore, it is important to have youth role-play the positive responses to situations discussed. Facilitators should always take the opposing (antagonist) role to provide youth participants with every opportunity to rehearse the prosocial responses.

In conclusion, it is essential that the program be employed only as one component to a wide range of sophisticated community strategies to address the complex problem of violence in relationships. In this way, it is consistent with, and exemplifies, the goals and objectives of the program by extending beyond itself and forging links with community services, women's advocates, and antiviolence initiatives in the community. The involvement of women's advocates who represent the voices of abused women and who have been the leaders in antiviolence work will enhance program development and promote the integrity of accountability within a program. Through building alliances and involving youth directly in community efforts, a strong and safety-conscious antiviolence initiative will flourish. In the beginning stages of networking in the area of woman abuse, one can expect to be challenged with a steep learning curve in terms of the issue and ongoing self-examination. To stay with the discomfort is to stay where the learning is, and to embrace the voices of youth in this work represents a significant contribution to violence prevention.

The Youth Relationships Project
London, Ontario

Acknowledgments

We would like to thank the many individuals and organizations who have given their time and resources to the development of this project and program manual. Without such commitment and tireless energy, this endeavor would not have progressed to its current state of knowledge and direction.

The Institute for the Prevention of Child Abuse deserves tremendous praise for its original commitment during the pilot phase of this project to the development of a prevention program to serve the wide needs of children and youth. Their start-up support permitted us to try out new ideas and take the initiative to structure a program that is truly *by youth and for youth*.

The formation of the ideas and procedures reflected throughout this project was intricately tied to the interests and support provided by the London/Middlesex Children's Aid Society. John Liston (Executive Director), Judy Van Leeuwen (Director of Intake and Child Abuse Services), Terry West (Director of Human Resources and Administration), and Judith Goldberg (Board Chair) lent their services and expertise to us during the critical formative stages of the project. Gary Price deserves special mention for his efforts at taking some rather uncertain thoughts and guidelines and turning them into workable plans to assist young people. Through his initial efforts, we built the community and group infrastructure that formed the program core.

The cooperation and assistance of the many social workers, teachers, and students is greatly appreciated. Many have implemented this program in their communities and schools and provided feedback for restructuring this manual. We extend a sincere thank you to the following people: Paul Ballantyne, Kim Smith, Wendy Rhindress, Bruce Burbank, John Mediema, Lorne Mann, Wendy Carron, Denis Campeau, Gary Price, Adele Lasuita, Nicole Neathway, Helen Kerr, Nancy O'Shea, Pam Lahn, Pam Bovey, Fred Holden, Katreena Scott, Andrea McEachran, and Janet O'Reilly.

We wish to thank Karen Bumstead of the Middlesex County Board of Education and Linda Crossley of the London Board of Education for their ardent efforts at implementing pilot groups in their schools.

The YRP Advisory Committee has been very helpful in establishing protocols for the program and providing assistance in establishing this program in the community, particularly in London,

Oxford County, and St. Thomas. We are especially grateful to Maureen Reid of London/Middlesex Children's Aid Society (CAS), Bob Pittman of Oxford County CAS, and Karen Shaw of St. Thomas Family and Children's Services for embracing this program so enthusiastically in their respective CAS agencies. The support of the Ontario Association of Children's Aid's Societies (OACAS) has been pivotal in establishing this program in many other CAS agencies in Ontario, including Toronto, Brantford, Huron County, and Perth County.

We have been fortunate to have been financially supported by organizations that place a high priority on the prevention of violence against women and children. Gordon Phaneuf, Program Development Consultant at Health Canada (Family Violence Prevention Division), took the initiative (and gamble) to fund the development of this manual, during a time when the economy was putting innovative programs such as this one on the back burner. We are indebted to his, and the division's, rapid and helpful assistance in keeping this project alive and well.

The Lawson Foundation also came along at a time in the development of this program when funding was critical. The foundation's advice and encouragement led us to receive crucial financial resources to ensure that the project had an evaluative, as well as a service, component. We also thank members of the local chapter of the Imperial Order of Daughters of the Empire (I.O.D.E.) and the May Court Club for their generous donations to assist in costs incurred in the transportation of youth participants and refreshments.

We would like to specially recognize the Ontario Mental Health Foundation (OMHF) for its Senior Research Fellowship Award to the principal investigator, which released David Wolfe from other obligations and thus freed the time necessary to turn his attention more fully to the project. Most recently, the OMHF also granted support for the research evaluation of this project over a 2-year period.

Most important, we thank the youths, their families, and their social workers who participated in the development of the pilot efforts and ongoing program evaluation. We have enjoyed getting to know the needs and concerns of young persons who face numerous obstacles in their pursuit of rewarding, violence-free relationships. They have taught us most of what constitutes this project's orientation and the weekly materials and discussion topics. We have attempted to listen and learn as well as to advise and teach, and we acknowledge the contribution of our many participants in helping us to communicate these methods to others.

The Youth Relationships Project (YRP)

PART

I

How to Use
This Manual

How to Use This Manual

Philosophy and Goals of the Project

Adolescence is a period of development in which many of the risk factors relating to interpersonal violence, stemming both from childhood as well as from contemporaneous sources, become more pronounced. Yet, adolescence has been substantially ignored in terms of its dynamic importance in establishing a pattern of healthy, nonviolent relationships with intimate partners and future family members.

Adolescence also encompasses important learning opportunities and successful accomplishments that far outweigh the discriminatory view of young people as being antisocial or violent. For these reasons, we need to seek ways to work *with* youth to assist them in forming choices and in learning nonviolent means of communicating with their current and future partners. From a developmental perspective, the transitional nature and normal disequilibrium that accompany adolescent development may represent an especially sensitive and opportune time for early intervention and enhancement experiences. From a societal perspective, an increasing demand for more long-lasting solutions is being echoed by more and more policymakers, professionals, and community groups as they become disillusioned with punitive strategies for dealing with youth crime and other forms of adolescent deviance (Millstein, Peterson, & Nightingale, 1993).

Helping young people to understand the abuse of power and control in their own relationships, so they may choose egalitarian relationships, is an approachable goal. We have developed a youth-centered educational program to assist young men to identify and to express feelings assertively, to recognize and respect the personal rights of female partners, and to own responsibility for their behavior. In addition, our program assists young women in understanding their personal rights, how to take care of their own safety, and how to express themselves assertively. With a greater understanding of the roots of violence, it becomes easier to recognize that preventing violence means not only stopping something unwanted from occurring—it also means providing adequate resources and increasing our commitment to youth and families.

Ours is a proactive, competency-enhancement approach rather than a "treatment." This program was designed to build strengths, resilience, and coping skills among youth as a way of enhancing interpersonal functioning. Every aspect of the program, from the material presented to the relationships between facilitators and participants, is designed to model appropriate use of power and to support youth empowerment.

A Conceptual Model of Intervention

The Youth Relationships Project, in addressing the contexts of violence, equalizes the issue of violence as one that can potentially affect all youth, albeit likely affecting some youth more than others. One way to capture the broad and complex process of violence in relationships is to consider violence as a funnel, moving from more general contexts that affect all youth (like media messages promoting relationships violence) to more specific contexts that carry a greater impact for "vulnerable" youth (like a violent social network for a given youth). This funnel is depicted in Figure I.1.

At the broadest level is the influence of living in a violent society. Society's subtle and tacit acceptance of violence and power imbalances affect all youth. Social themes like "might is right," "she got what was coming to her," and "sex sells" are reflective of societal levels of violence that perpetuate negative stereotypes and adversarial and hostile views toward others (especially women) and set the stage for harm toward others. Male superiority and female passivity are common themes among popular cultural depictions about the genders in their relationships. These influences are seen in childhood icons as well as youth subculture. In a *New York Times Magazine* article, Pollitt (1991) relates her observations:

> Little girls learn to split their consciousness, filtering their dreams and ambitions through boy characters while admiring the clothes of the princess. The more privileged and daring can dream of becoming exceptional women in a man's world—Smurfettes. The others are being taught to accept the more usual fate, which is to be a passenger car drawn through life by a masculine train engine. Boys, who are rarely confronted with stories in which males play only minor roles, learn a simpler lesson: girls just don't matter much. (p. 24)

A more specific level as we flow down the funnel is the impact of violence in the family, affecting a narrower range of individuals in society. Although in many homes significant levels of maltreatment are disrupting a child's ability to form positive, healthy relationships, many more families may be limiting a child's ability to maximize his or her relationships through traditional socializa-

FUNNEL OF VIOLENCE

Living in a Violent Culture

Living in a Violent Family

Living with Violent Peers and Partners

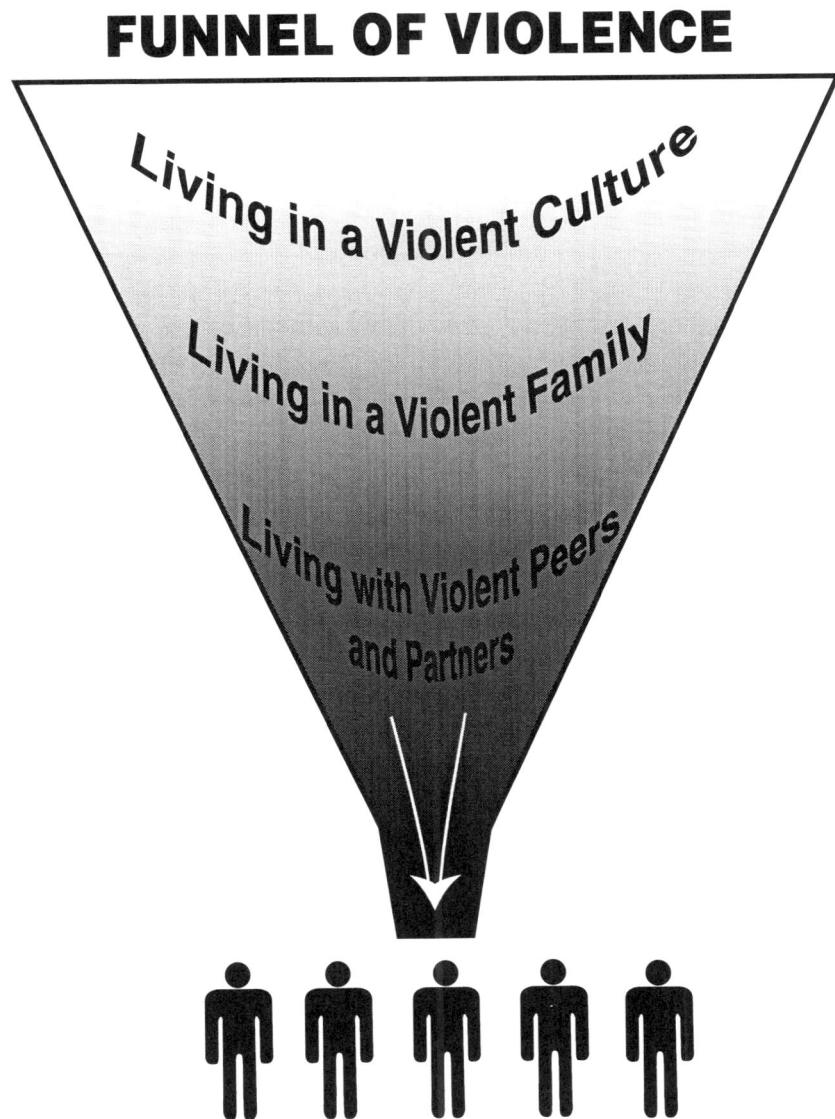

Figure I.1. Funnel Diagram

tion practices that promote inequality among the genders. Normative socialization practices often promote rigid gender roles for four children: Boys are raised to be strong, silent "doers," and girls are raised to be quiet but compassionate, backseat "helpers." Research has found that when preschool age boys are given stereotypic toys, they very often have strong reactions.

> During the session they tried to do anything but play with the cross-sex toys. One boy flung the doll across the room and turned his back on it, getting it at least out of his sight if not out of mind. Some sought to restructure their limited options by sticking to the moderately sex-typed material

and transforming it into masculine tools, as for example, using beaters in the cooking set as guns or drills. (Bussey & Bandura, 1992, p. 1247)

Toward the bottom of the funnel, the youth's interactions with peers and partners serve to reinforce all that has come before. Increasingly, researchers have found support for the view that "birds of a feather flock together." Vulnerable youths are more likely to associate with other vulnerable youths. This can almost be empowering, contributing to a clear sense of identity and familiar connection. Although the Youth Relationships Project is appropriate to all youth, we feel it has a special importance to these vulnerable youth.

A key construct for understanding interpersonal violence is the power imbalance necessary for abusive behavior and victimization to occur (Dutton, 1995; Pence & Paymar, 1993; Walker, 1989). Our model addresses both sides of the issue of the abuse of power and control—offending behavior and victimization experiences— for both males and females. Also, the current model targets negative behaviors to be prevented as well as desired behaviors to be promoted. Relationships are considered in terms of aspects that increase the risk of violence as well as behavior that promotes egalitarian problem solving. Although early maltreatment and negative relationship patterns are strong predeterminants of coercive physical and sexual behavior (both as victim and as victimizer) in young adulthood, we argue that the developmental course can be mediated through psychoeducational intervention during adolescence that involves the following components: (a) cognitive awareness of the foundations of abusive behavior and attitudes and beliefs about relationship violence, (b) skills to help adolescents build healthy relationships and to recognize and respond to abuse in their own relationships and in relationships of their peers, and (c) community-based problem solving to increase competency through community involvement and social action.

Fisher and Fisher (1992) conclude in their review of risk prevention programs with adolescents that modification of "risk behaviors" is best achieved by attending simultaneously to participants' needs for accurate information, motivational influences, and behavioral skills. Coupled with the theoretical factors linked to relationship violence noted above, we have based our conceptual framework for intervention on these three intervention components. This prevention model was also developed in conjunction with other health promotion efforts with young people, such as for sexual activity, weight control, smoking, and exercise, in which considerable progress has been made by capitalizing on the natural interest and motivation of teens to learn about lifestyle issues (Dryfoos, 1990). For example, Millstein et al. (1993) describe major considerations for health promotion with young people: (a) Greater self-understanding can be fostered through

Table I.1. Aims and Objectives of the Youth Relationships Project

Intervention Aims and Constructs	*Intervention Objectives (Sessions)*
Section A: "Violence in Close Relationships: It's All About Power" *Aim 1:* Understanding power and its role in relationship violence *Constructs:* Power and control; myths about abuse; personal power and safety; communication	1. Establishing a safe, teen-centered environment 2. Power in relationships: explosions and assertions 3. Defining relationship violence: power abuses
Section B: "Breaking the Cycle of Violence: What We Can Choose to Do and What We Can Choose Not to Do" *Aim 2:* Developing skills needed to help adolescents build healthy relationships and to recognize and respond to abuse in their own relationships *Constructs:* Role stereotypes; choosing partners; sexism	4. Defining powerful relationships: equality, empathy, and emotional expressiveness 5. Defining powerful relationships: assertiveness instead of aggressiveness 6. Understanding power processes: victim and batterer
Section C: "The Contexts of Relationship Violence" *Aim 3:* To understand the societal influences and pressures that can lead to violence and to develop skills to respond to these influences *Constructs:* Sexism; gender differences; media influences; assertiveness	7. Peer pressure and the case of date rape 8. Gender socialization and societal pressures 9. Choosing partners and sex role stereotypes 10. Sexism 11. Media and sexism
Section D: "Making a Difference: Working Toward Breaking the Cycle of Violence" *Aim 4:* Increasing competency through community involvement and social action *Constructs:* Help seeking; community action	12. Confronting sexism and violence against women 13. Getting to know community helpers for relationship violence 14-16. Getting out and about in the community 17. Social action event 18. End of group celebration

interventions in which youth learn to express personal points of view while keeping an open mind to alternative perspectives; (b) active exploration of alternative roles can be supported by community-based projects, apprenticeships, and other learning experiences; (c) teens may build self-esteem by experiencing opportunities to feel competent and behave successfully; (d) self-efficacy and potency are bolstered by improving their life skills and providing opportunity for community service; and (e) support from peers can be increased by interventions or educational opportunities aimed at these social-cognitive behavioral skills. These considerations were woven into the aims and objectives shown in Table I.1.

Intended Participants

This project targets the prevention of violence against women, focusing on male and female adolescents between 14 and 16 years old (please see the following section detailing the rationale for targeting this age group). We have focused our attention primarily on those who have lived with violence and abuse in the past, although the program does not require such prerequisite experiences. In fact, we prefer not to *select* a particular youth for the program but to open the program to any interested teen, whether or not he or she has been involved in a dating relationship.

This minimal selection process serves two important functions: First, an open-ended policy avoids the negative labeling that so often occurs when a youth is referred for services. Second, because the program is preventive in nature, we wish to reach young people *before* they have become involved in a violent relationship. Although participants have generally been involved in some degree of relationship conflict and/or abuse, such behavior is by no means an inclusionary or exclusionary requirement for participation. Program organizers may, however, wish to exclude an individual from the program if he or she has other needs that preempt the benefits of involvement in the YRP program. These needs might include the following concerns (and each individual should be carefully screened through an intake interview to ensure suitability of the program):

- Life-threatening medical illness or chronic neurological illness
- IQ below 75
- Previous incarceration stemming from criminal charges for a crime against persons (e.g., sexual assault, mugging) since age 12
- Not available to attend for 18 weeks
- Residential treatment or hospitalization within past year for *DSM-IV*-related disorder
- Extreme acting-out behaviors

Implementing the Program

Group Structure and Operation

The YRP was designed to be conducted on a weekly basis with small groups of male and female youths (ranging from a bare minimum of 8 to a maximum of 15). Each session lasts 2 hours, with a planned break in the middle. *We feel it is very important that the program be conducted in full, without eliminating any objectives or content, to ensure that the integrity of the program is preserved.*

Because the program content builds on previous knowledge and skills, the order of delivery was carefully determined. Most important, we find that teens benefit most when they are able to invest the time and energy required to build trust and commitment. For example, the social action component of the program involves participants in community activities aimed at ending violence against women and preserving their commitment to this cause, and it requires more outreach on the part of both the facilitators as well as the youths. Without this component, however, maintenance of the gains may be lost. *We urge potential facilitators to maintain the fullness of the program to ensure that the issue receives the time and involvement necessary to effect change.*

Establishing a "teen-centered" environment is also essential to the success of a group program on violence prevention. More important than the content of information and skills is the integrity of the facilitators in their honesty and their modeling of noncontrolling communication. Program staff should clearly outline the purpose of the group and present the information they will cover during the course of their time together. They should frame a group agreement around what the *youths* want in order to create a safe environment and to discuss sensitive and sometimes personal information. Thus, at the outset of the group, the facilitators must acknowledge directly the power and privilege they hold; although facilitators present information and help guide discussions, the group belongs to the young people. The facilitators will not punish or try to control but will support what the group chooses to do in response to disruptive behavior or problems that arise during the group.

Using the Program in Schools

Although the Youth Relationships Project was originally developed as an after-school program, it is possible for groups to be conducted within a school setting and as part of the educational curriculum. Adopting the program for school use allows for large numbers of young people to benefit from its goals and objectives. There are some special considerations, however, if facilitators choose to run the program within this framework.

First and foremost, the youths' voluntary commitment to the group is essential. Unfortunately, if group participation is required for course credit or if school staff select youth for the program, the element of voluntary consent is lost. In the past, we have found that this seriously detracts from the success of the group and from the extent to which the teens individually benefit from the program. Therefore, we strongly urge that schools work to ensure that no youth joins the group if he or she would otherwise choose not to attend.

Second, each session requires 2 hours for completion. It is possible to split each session in half so that the group may be run during class hours. However, because each session has specific goals and objectives and because each exercise within the session builds on those completed previously, facilitators will face the added challenge of maintaining each session's integrity. Offering the program as an after-school option is an alternative to working the session content into class hours.

Third, schools must carefully consider their choice of group cofacilitators. Because the success of the program depends heavily on community participation and involvement, we do recommend that at least one, if not both, of the program facilitators come from relevant community agencies that work to end woman abuse. This is an important way of connecting the youths to the community and the community to the youths. In the past, teens have been especially receptive to "outside" facilitators whose presence demonstrates an obvious commitment to the program, who bring new information to the group, and with whom they can develop a unique relationship.

Alternatively, groups have been run with available and qualified school staff. Using school staff has some advantage in that teens have an added opportunity to build a lasting relationship with that person. However, the program also encourages sharing of personal information and this may not be comfortable for either staff or student. Furthermore, because the role modeling of egalitarian relationships is so important to this program, teachers are asked to play a role that is very different than that generally associated with classroom settings. For example, everyone in the group is asked to use their first names, and teachers may not be comfortable with this approach, especially if they have the same students in other classes. Teens are also given a great deal of responsibility in this program (as in setting the group rules and ensuring that they are followed), and teachers may find it difficult to adopt a "hands-off" approach to discipline in the group and a "hands-on" approach with the same students in other classes. *If a school staff member is selected as a program facilitator, she or he should acknowledge and address these concerns with the youth participants, and invite the students to do the same.* Honesty about one's feelings is a fundamental tenet of this program.

We also encourage potential facilitators of this program to see our project staff as a resource, and hope that they will contact our office with their questions and concerns about running this program within a school setting.

Setting Up the Program in Your Community

To ensure successful implementation of this program, there is some legwork to be done in the community prior to commencement of the program. Many guidelines to community participation have been included in the manual. You will be looking to the community for support and assistance when searching for guest speakers and visiting community agencies. Sending community agencies a flyer or memo outlining the program is recommended. We also suggest that people who facilitate this group program be community social workers who are familiar with youth issues and the issues of woman abuse. To provide a community perspective versus an agency perspective, it is preferred that the facilitators come from two different community agencies.

Near the beginning of the program, there is an opportunity for the youths to hear about the experiences of a victim of woman abuse and a former abuser. This has been a very effective means of providing reality and immediacy to the issue for the young people. Finding people willing to speak to these issues in your community may be difficult without the support of battered women's advocacy agencies and men's counseling programs. Included in this manual are protocols that have been endorsed by the London Coordinating Committee to End Woman Abuse in our community. These protocols outline the role, purpose, and responsibilities of speakers in this program. This information will be helpful in explaining your request when looking for speakers.

If suitable speakers cannot be obtained in your community, advocates from women's and men's counseling programs would be acceptable alternatives.

In Section D, "Making a Difference," teens will be going out into the community to learn about the agencies that can be of assistance to them when they are looking for help. We recommend phone calls and letters to these agencies describing the program and purpose of this exercise. Their understanding and cooperation will ease the facilitation of this section. We appreciate that community social service agencies are very busy; however, their assistance and cooperation in this section of the program is very meaningful for the teens. It is often their first opportunity to see the services available in their community. Remember, one of these agencies may be the lucky recipient of funds raised from the teens' social action project!

Cofacilitator Qualities and Characteristics

The Youth Relationships Project offers a unique opportunity to teenagers who have experienced violence in their lives or who are at risk for violence in future interpersonal relationships. This opportunity is made available to youths through a series of 18 weekly group meetings *that are led by both a male and a female cofacilitator.* Because the cofacilitators are the mediums through which the information is being learned, the skills rehearsed, and the discussion and skill implementation facilitated, their role is crucial. Listed below are a number of characteristics and qualities that we consider to be important for the success of a Youth Relationships Project Teen Group facilitator. *We ask that all potential cofacilitators carefully consider whether they are open to this project approach, and whether they have the necessary skills, attitudes, and philosophies to run a YRP group.*

Abilities

• *A good understanding and working knowledge of the causes and effects of woman abuse*

Cofacilitators must have a solid understanding of the causes and effects of woman abuse, especially in terms of its connections to sexism, power, and control.

• *A clear understanding of the goals and philosophy of the YRP*

The YRP staff share this responsibility and will ease this learning through a training workshop and/or the provision of training materials. However, it is also the responsibility of the cofacilitators to thoroughly familiarize themselves with the program manual and to pay special attention to the section on YRP goals and philosophies. If a person has any major difficulties with the goals and philosophical approach adopted by the YRP, that person may not be an appropriate facilitator for this program.

• *A strong commitment to the group for the full 18 sessions*

Facilitating this kind of teen group for 18 sessions is a time-consuming task, and it is important that facilitators be realistic about what their schedules allow. Although the group itself lasts 2 hours per week, facilitators can expect to spend an additional 3 hours a week with planning and organization. Cofacilitators should be willing to read the program manual in its entirety before starting the group. This includes previewing videos and practicing role-plays to become familiar and comfortable with the information and the format in which it is to be presented.

• *Good organizational and planning skills*

In addition to keeping track of 10 to 14 teenagers, this group requires coordination with outside community agencies for in-house speaking engagements, agency visits, and social action opportunities. Cofacilitators therefore should have the necessary skills and abilities to plan well in advance and to keep on top of several different activities at once!

• *The ability to work well in partnership with the cofacilitator, the teens in the group, and the project staff*

The YRP runs very much by the philosophy that we are far more effective together than alone. It is important that a cofacilitator views the other cofacilitator, the teens, and the project staff as rich sources of information and that he or she is willing to use the cofacilitator and the project staff as support systems—and they can rely on him or her for the same. We believe that the ability to share roles and responsibilities is important to any group effort. This is particularly important to a project in which the goal is to promote healthy, mutual, supportive, and strong interpersonal relationships.

• *Previous experience working with teen groups may be an asset but is not a requirement and is not a sufficient qualification by itself*

More often than not, we learn through experience. As such, previous experience participating in or facilitating a group may offer some advantage to potential cofacilitators for this group. However, this group also runs on a philosophy that is very different than more traditional structures, such that we may be asking facilitators to "unlearn" tactics used in different settings. We hope that facilitators who have experience working in group settings will spend some time thinking about what they liked about previous groups, what they would do differently, and how the philosophy of that group fits with the philosophy of the YRP. We hope that potential cofacilitators with no previous group experience will spend time asking the same questions of those who have had this kind of experience.

Qualities

The following list of cofacilitator qualities focuses on the kinds of attitude and belief systems that we believe fit well with our model. Although these qualities are not necessarily demonstrable skills or behaviors, they are reflective of a certain attitude that will clearly communicate itself to the teens in the group.

• *Ownership of one's social and personal power in the group and in the broader social context*

Primarily, cofacilitators need to acknowledge their personal and social power. Social power stems from membership in certain social groups (e.g., being white, male, adult, middle or upper class, heterosexual, able-bodied). Personal power comes from personal attributes that may or may not stem from social group membership. Being comfortable talking in a large group and being particularly effective at winning an argument are two examples of personal power that could be misused or taken advantage of if not acknowledged and owned. Therefore, cofacilitators need to examine the ways in which the presence and absence of social and personal power function in their day-to-day lives.

• *Responsibility for one's social and personal power and privilege*

Beyond the acknowledgment of social and personal power, each person must make a commitment to be responsible for the power and privilege in his or her life. According to each person's background, he or she will hold different kinds of social and personal power and privilege. As cofacilitators, however, you will all be inherently more powerful than the youths in the group. You will be responsible for disseminating information, the way it is expressed, who gets to respond to it, and so on. Although we make suggestions as to ways in which you can minimize an authoritarian, hierarchical group structure, the reality is that you will have more power than the young people. Cofacilitators must be able to show teens how to have power *and* be responsible for it.

• *Concordance between the attitudes, beliefs, and behavior expressed within the group and those you express outside the group*

Although it is an incredible challenge to live one's life by the principles one espouses, we are looking for cofacilitators who can be genuine when expressing principles of nonviolence, mutuality, and responsibility during group discussions. It is our hope that a teen could see you in a different setting and see how the attitudes, beliefs, and behaviors expressed during the group are maintained outside the group.

• *A strong sense of personal safety skills, limits, and boundaries*

Although this project uses a competency enhancement rather than a treatment approach, many teens will be struggling with difficult and often painful personal experiences of violence. They may choose to share some of these experiences with the group, and it is crucial that facilitators are prepared to handle personal disclosures. This begins with a strong sense of your own safety skills, a sense of respect for your boundaries, and an honest acknowledgment of your limits.

• *An acute awareness of ways in which both verbal and non-verbal behaviors communicate messages to teenagers*

From the minute you first meet the teenagers, you will act as a role model for them. Your verbal and nonverbal behaviors will be the clearest indication of your underlying attitudes and values. Cofacilitators need to be very conscious of the subtle and not-so-subtle messages they may be sending to other people. For example, do you have a habit of interrupting? How do you handle it when somebody interrupts you? What messages does your body language communicate? Cofacilitators must be open and willing to examine their own behaviors throughout this process.

• *A willingness to challenge your "comfort zones" and step outside roles in which you normally function*

At the end of each session, we ask cofacilitators to take some time to consider whether they felt the facilitation was equally shared, and whether or not the teens would perceive the facilitation to be equally shared. This may be a challenge to some because we often find our particular strengths and stick to them. We are therefore looking for cofacilitators who are willing to challenge themselves to adopt roles that may be new and unfamiliar, and often uncomfortable at the onset.

• *A willingness to learn from the group and to challenge your own attitudes, beliefs, and behaviors*

We hope that facilitating this kind of a teen group will be as much a learning opportunity for you as it will be for the teens. Cofacilitators usually see this project as an opportunity to learn more about themselves, their interactions with others, and their social interactions. As such, we prefer cofacilitators who will welcome a challenge and will push themselves beyond their current limits.

• *A willingness to give youth power and control in a group setting*

This includes providing youth with the opportunity to take on leadership roles during group sessions and to plan and facilitate portions of the weekly sessions. Cofacilitators will allow teens to explore together and independently for answers to questions, rather than providing them with the "correct answers."

• *A willingness to relax, have fun, and enjoy the opportunity*

Cofacilitators who think they might genuinely enjoy working with a group of teenagers for 18 sessions are most welcome! We want to ensure that this group is as much a positive experience for you as it is for the teens.

Establishing a "teen-centered" environment is also essential to the success of a group program on violence prevention. More important than the content of information and skills is the integrity of the facilitators in their honesty and their modeling of noncontrolling communication. Program staff should clearly outline the purpose of the group and present the information they will cover during the course of their time together. They should frame a group agreement around what the *youths* want to create a safe environment and to discuss sensitive and sometimes personal information. Thus, at the outset of the group, the facilitators must acknowledge directly the power and privilege they hold; although facilitators present information and help guide discussions, the group belongs to the young people. The facilitators will not punish or try to control but will support what the group chooses to do in response to disruptive behavior or problems that arise during the group.

Safety Awareness Concerning Young Women in the Program

A word of caution about the safety of female participants in the program: Initially, there was a concern that co-ed groups discussing and debating the issues related to violence against women could, in fact, be harmful to female participants. For example, a girl in the group who has an undisclosed history of victimization could be revictimized by male(s) in the group struggling with the issues and/or making jokes about the violence.

We have determined that because the program is offered in an educational forum rather than a counseling forum, delivery is similar to a classroom discussion on the issues. The group often involves personal disclosure, however, so it becomes essential to revisit the group agreement (e.g., respect of others) if jokes or minimizing occur in conjunction with an individual sharing personal experiences. It is also worthwhile to note that, based on statistical probability, many in the room will have experienced abuse, so it is important to reiterate the group agreement when sexist or belittling comments are made.

Male Defensiveness

We define male defensiveness as attitudes and behaviors that deny the significance of woman abuse in our society and that deny the gender context in which the abuse occurs. During the course of the group program, male defensiveness may arise from males and females in the group. The youths often feel uncomfortable with the assertions made regarding male responsibility for relationship violence. It is the most prevalent obstacle encountered when conducting groups that attempt to explore and change men's violence toward women.

Male defensiveness can be expressed in many different forms. It can be subtle and include behaviors such as inappropriate laughter, snickering, attempts to distract other youth, or general negative comments about the activity being "dumb." When this happens, it's a good idea to check out the possibility that some of the youths are feeling uncomfortable with the focus on men's violence. Remember, the cofacilitators' willingness to address these feelings directly role models for the teens the importance of clear and honest communication.

Alternatively, male defensiveness may be expressed directly. Listed below are some typical questions posed during the group that reflect feelings of male defensiveness. Also provided are a number of possible responses to these questions. However, *it is important to try to reflect questions back to the group. Try to avoid fostering debates between the cofacilitators and the youths.* This works most effectively by trying to get the teens to answer their own questions.

Why are men always blamed?

- "Men are blamed because most violence is committed by males and because men are socialized to be aggressive."
- Try and focus the discussion on the problem of violence instead of on the issue of blame (i.e., What needs to be done?).

Don't women sometimes provoke or deserve the abuse?

- "Violence is never justified."
- Identify this as a victim-blaming tactic.

What about men who are battered?

- "It does happen and it's not OK either; however, the overwhelming majority of victims of relationship violence are women."
- "Men are typically larger and stronger and more likely to injure women."
- "Men have greater access to financial and other resources, so they are less likely to be trapped in an abusive relationship."

Why would women stay or go back to an abusive partner? Doesn't this mean the violence is not a problem?

- "It's hard for women to leave because of poverty, isolation, lack of support, having nowhere to go, possibly not getting full custody of their children, and so on."
- "Women have realistic fears of retaliation (most women who are killed by their partners are killed postseparation)."
- "The woman's partner may promise that he will change or that he can't survive without her."

Isn't most violence caused by alcohol or drug use?

- "Alcohol may make violence worse, but removing alcohol does not solve the problem of violence against women."
- "Not all men who are violent and abusive abuse drugs or alcohol."
- "Women report that batterers who do abuse drugs and alcohol are also violent when sober."

If the issue of male defensiveness is not addressed openly, honestly, and in a supportive manner, it can take up a lot of time and energy and detract from the youths' opportunity to learn throughout the group. It's important to thank the teens for being honest about how they are feeling and let them know that it's OK to bring up these thoughts whenever they occur throughout the group.

Development of the Youth Relationships Project

Development of the Youth Relationships Project

The need to develop effective prevention and educational strategies to reduce or eliminate violence against women and children is critical. Approximately 3 to 4 million American households and 500,000 Canadian households experience a significant degree of violence directed at women and/or children every year (Statistics Canada, 1993; Straus & Gelles, 1990). Woman abuse has become the leading cause of injuries to women aged 15 to 44—more common than auto accidents, muggings, and cancer deaths combined (U.S. Senate Judiciary Committee, 1992). Child abuse, moreover, is the leading cause of injuries to small children and the leading cause of death among infants and toddlers (U.S. Advisory Board on Child Abuse and Neglect, 1990). Rape affects a sizable proportion of adult women, and for those under the age of 35 years, rape is feared even more than murder. Sexual abuse of girls and boys has also emerged as a common occurrence, believed to affect 27% of females and 16% of males in the course of their childhood (Finkelhor, Hotaling, Lewis, & Smith, 1990). For girls, sexual abuse by someone that she knows in her family is more common than any other type of assault or injury.

Despite these prominent findings, North American society has been generally slow to grasp the scope or seriousness of violence against women and children, and even slower to develop ways to deter its occurrence.

The current project grew from the recognition that violence against women and children has its roots in similar developmental processes and sociocultural experiences. Thus it is perhaps not surprising to find common themes emerging across studies of the backgrounds and psychological profiles of sexual and physical abusers of women and children. For example, Wolfe (1994) noted that sexual and physical offenders of women and children overlap in their *demographic descriptions* (i.e., lower educational achievement, history of parental criminal activity, lower occupational status, male), in their *developmental backgrounds* (i.e., poor attachment relationships, multiple forms of abuse and violence, significant developmental disruptions), in their *personality features* (i.e., lifestyle deviance, limited emotional and behavioral control, social isolation, intimacy problems), and in their *manner of resolving current conflicts/arousal* (i.e., physiological arousal is more often followed by distorted beliefs regarding why they are upset or sexually aroused and who is responsible).

Given the prominent similarities in the backgrounds, personalities, and behavioral expression of *known* offenders against women and children, we embarked on a search to understand more about the processes involved along the way in the formation of violent attitudes and behavior. We were informed initially by the clinical and empirical recognition that many offenders seemed to be repeating patterns of behavior that were very similar to what they had experienced. Similarly, we recognized that many children and adults who were harmed by these individuals had to overcome significant injuries to both their physical and their psychological makeup—which in some instances could last a lifetime.

We presumed that these intergenerational patterns could be influenced through a concerted effort to inform youth (mostly young men) of the abuses of power and control and provide them with more understanding and skill in nonviolent forms of communication. Similarly, we presumed that young women, whether they had been the direct victims of an abusive relationship or not, could benefit from greater knowledge in terms of self-awareness, self-protection, and intolerance for sexual and physical forms of harassment and abuse, coupled with greater skill at self-assertion and effective communication.

Although recognizing that these gender-based issues are grounded in our broader socialization processes as well as individual family patterns, we felt that adolescence represents a transitional time in the formation of youths' own intimate relationships wherein they would be interested in and receptive to ideas and knowledge about the workings of healthy, nonviolent relationships. We were extremely pleased at the response from young people to this approach, which led us to the formation of this program manual.

Beginnings

In 1989, the Institute for the Prevention of Child Abuse (IPCA) in Toronto, Ontario, Canada, hosted a conference to discuss expert opinion on the best ways to prevent child abuse, with the intention of launching a longitudinal study in the near future (see Starr & Wolfe, 1991, for a full discussion of these papers). After 2 days of discussion, the general consensus from this conference involving 20 recognized experts in the field was that the best windows of opportunity seem to be during pregnancy and postnatal delivery/child care, and during adolescence. The rationale for the former window of opportunity is well known; parents, especially new parents, need all the help they can get when learning about their role and the needs of their child. It is at this formative point in time when parents who lack sensitive and appropriate ways of relating to their children are most willing to learn and to receive advice and assistance (Wekerle & Wolfe, 1993).

Adolescence, on the other hand, is often viewed as being somewhat removed from child care responsibilities and concerns about future interests in children, much less future child abuse. However, the group of experts discussed the value of educating and preparing youth during this important transitional period in which dating and peer relationships and interpersonal style become firmly established. Violence prevention, it can be reasoned, could be attempted during adolescence if one accepts the view that youth are setting the stage for their established relationship patterns later on, and may benefit from experiences involving dependency roles and/or nontraditional roles (especially if the teens had experienced abusive or inappropriate child care and were thus ill-prepared to enter into healthy, noncoercive relationships).

Based on this conference, the IPCA Research Committee discussed directions they wanted to pursue toward the prevention of child abuse in future generations. The committee supported our research team to embark on some of the directions discussed at the conference and to develop a pilot study to look at ways of working with adolescents. The current ongoing project and program manual described herein are the result of this 4-year endeavor.

Initially, we attempted to design this program expressly for adolescent *males*, based on the existing rationale that males at risk of violence (due to their own violent backgrounds) become the next perpetrators. Furthermore, we believed that little was being done to work with such individuals *prior to* the commission of an offense. The research committee explored the needs of males at child protective services (CPS) by forming small pilot groups and raising issues related to violence in relationships. Although our initial intent was to work with males only, the teens told us that they would prefer to attend the program if girls their own age were present. They were (understandably) more interested in their current dating and social relationships. This "reality check" led to prominent changes in our focus toward the development of healthy relationships among youth and the expansion of the program to include young women as well as young men.

Youth-Focused, Action-Learning Strategy

We began our initial group discussions with the philosophy that teens must have a prominent say in how information is chosen and delivered, and they must have ample opportunities to discuss and rehearse any new information or skills. Our initial pilot groups led to the formation of the three principal sections of the program: (a) informational, (b) skills-based, and (c) social action-learning opportunities.

In terms of information, we found that the young people first of all needed to gain a basic understanding of "healthy and unhealthy relationships," how violence and abuse affect themselves and others, and what alternatives exist in resolving conflicts and avoiding the repeated cycle of coercion and abuse.

For skill development, we acknowledged that the teens needed to observe how others handle conflict, arousal, or debate without resorting to power-based solutions or ineffective forms of communication. To this end, a series of exercises dealing with communication skills and conflict resolution skills were developed.

Finally, we understood from the literature that youth benefit most from prevention programs that build in ample opportunity for their own personal commitment and action (in this case, to end violence against women). The third segment of the program, therefore, developed into a community-based, hands-on experience in which participants are given an opportunity to practice solving "real problems" with "real people." As pairs, they receive a hypothetical problem situation and go about finding ways in the community to receive help and advice. We attempt, at this point, to act as consultants and make their approach to community persons as realistic, yet successful, as possible.

Having operated several pilot groups involving teens with backgrounds of maltreatment and poor family relationships, we produced the detailed curriculum and procedures contained herein. The evaluation of this program is ongoing, with long-term results concerning the prevention of violence and the formation of healthy relationships expected over several more years. Although still in its beginnings, we have found the response of the participants as well as the community to be promising and worthwhile. We are encouraged by the pilot findings to date (e.g., Wolfe, Wekerle, Gough, & Reitzel, 1993; Wolfe, Wekerle, McEachran, et al., 1995) and have begun dissemination and long-term evaluation of this endeavor.

Evaluation

Evaluation of the Youth Relationships Project is an ongoing process. We began to evaluate the impact of our program in 1992 following the completion of our first "pilot" group of adolescents, and at the current time we are evaluating the program involving adolescents from several high schools and child protective service agencies. Because the long-range impact of the program, especially the preventive benefits, will require years of follow-up and detailed investigation, we are not currently in a position to draw scientific conclusions as to the merits of this program. We are encouraged, however, by the preliminary results of our investigation and wish to draw the attention of interested readers to the issues that need to be considered in conducting their own formal or informal evaluation of this approach.

An initial evaluation of our pilot efforts was presented at the annual conference of the American Psychological Association (Wolfe et al., 1993). We compared both sexes ($N = 19$ girls and $N = 16$ boys) of participants on our principal dimensions of conflict resolution, sexual coercion and victimization, behavioral adjustment, and past experiences of maltreatment. First, we noted that the girls in our pilot sample were more behaviorally malad-justed than the normal population, which is not surprising given that they were chosen from a protective service population. Accordingly, girls were elevated on the child behavior checklist, and they reported more sexual abuse in their past than did the boys. We also found that girls reported more use of blame statements during conflict situations, and were equally as high as boys on report of physical aggression/intimidation. However, girls also reported significantly more sexual victimization, compared with the amount of sexual coercion reported by the boys (in fact, most of these girls had experienced all major forms of sexual exploita-tion and violence).

We are currently conducting a full evaluation of the prevention program using improved methodology and measurement (see Wolfe et al., in press, for discussion of the program and pilot findings). We have modified our procedures to allow for more accurate screening and referral of participants, and have eliminated those measurement devices that were less sensitive to the issues being addressed. We have added new measures that permit multi-informant, multidimensional assessment of the cognitive and behavioral changes brought about by the intervention. Finally, we have added a 3½-year follow-up period (beyond the posttest assessment), which we believe will be adequate in demonstrating the maintenance of desired changes. Following the 4-year evaluation of this program, we plan to maintain contact with participants for the purpose of interviewing future partners to determine the long-term preventive impact of this violence preven-tion initiative.

Persons wishing to conduct their own formal evaluation of this program are encouraged to contact the Youth Relationships Proj-ect to discuss different measurement tools and evaluation objec-tives. Because the psychometric properties of the instruments developed for this project have not been fully evaluated, we are unable to disseminate these instruments at the current time; however, we are pleased to discuss evaluation goals and plans with different community and academic organizations who wish to conduct their own evaluation, in an attempt to provide the most up-to-date information about our measures and procedures. We encourage some form of evaluation to be done on an ongoing basis when using these materials, both for the purpose of refining the program as well as to determine the short- and long-range benefits and positive and negative side effects.

Finally, we have included our Participant Rating Form (see Appendix B), which is useful in conducting a process evaluation of weekly progress attained by each member, and our Group Participant Feedback Form (see Session 18), which is administered to participants at the end of the program to solicit their feedback about the material. Group leaders find such information from youths to be of considerable importance in adapting their style and delivery, and we have found the weekly ratings of participants (based on the observations of cofacilitators or assistants) to be useful in determining the rate of growth of each member across several important areas such as interest and motivation, participation in discussion, and understanding of material.

Preliminary Studies

Factors associated with increased risk of gender-based violence among high school students. Because this program targets low-frequency behaviors (i.e., physical and sexual abuse/harassment as well as prosocial development), most existing measurement tools are inadequate for evaluation purposes. Our theoretical model (see Wolfe, Wekerle, Reitzel-Jaffe, & Gough, 1995) comprises (a) preexisting risk factors (e.g., maltreatment history, attachment), (b) interpersonal sensitivity (e.g., hostility), and (c) personal resources (e.g., strategies in problem solving; attitudes and beliefs) as major factors affecting conflict and violence in teen relationships. We tested this model on a group of 359 high school students, both to determine the psychometric properties of our instruments as well as to test the strength of the model (see Wolfe, Wekerle, Reitzel-Jaffe, & Lefebvre, 1995).

The results of this study were very convincing on both accounts. The measures were reliable and capable of discriminating between the two samples of high- and low-risk students (risk was defined on the basis of their past maltreatment history). Findings also supported the hypothesis that history of maltreatment is associated with the theoretically identified risk factors; moreover, high-risk males and females both reported significantly more coercion and emotional abuse toward and by dating partners, compared with their low-risk counterparts.

Interaction between maltreatment history and attachment security. Part of what maltreatment may bring to relationships is an underlying conflictual, even violent, dynamic in which interactants are seen in terms of stark power differentials, with aggression and a sense of personal entitlement overlapping with the victimizer role, and passivity and a sense of personal deprivation overlapping with the victim role. A goal of this study was to examine the interaction between childhood maltreatment and current attachment style in predicting current conflict in relationships. Given that adolescence may present a bridge in relationship style from childhood to adulthood, adolescent relationships were targeted.

To test an interaction model, we entered maltreatment and attachment ratings singly into the equation, followed by the interaction of maltreatment and attachment ratings. Results confirmed the hypothesis that attachment and maltreatment combined are strong predictors of conflict in dating relationships, but this finding was predominately found *only for males.* For example, for the male sample, the interaction of maltreatment with enmeshment (problems with closeness) ratings, as well as the interaction of maltreatment with trust ratings, accounted for additional variance in predicting reports of coercion toward female dating partners (total $R^2 = .23, .33$, respectively; see Wekerle, Wolfe, & Lefebvre, 1995).

Pilot outcome study: Modeling growth as a function of psychoeducational intervention. The next step of our preliminary evaluation was to determine the level of interest and understanding shown by young people who participate, and to measure their growth in these areas over time as a function of the program. A growth modeling analysis was used in a study to demonstrate the degree of interest, motivation, and understanding shown by teens at risk of relationship violence across the weeks of their involvement in our program (Wolfe, Wekerle, McEachran, et al., 1995). Using a multiwave approach (i.e., weekly ratings of change), each individual growth trajectory was represented mathematically by a linear growth model to describe true status as a function of time (Willett, Ayoub, & Robinson, 1991). The straight line growth model applied herein looked at one key growth parameter: the slope of each line, which represented weekly rate of change for each participant. The purpose of this pilot study was to examine growth in the skills and behaviors targeted both to increase (e.g., positive problem solving, assertiveness) and to decrease (e.g., controlling or dominating behavior, negative problem solving) over the 18-week sessions described in the current manual, using weekly facilitator ratings.

Thirty youths (16 females, 14 males) between the ages of 13 and 16 years inclusive ($M = 14.7$), who were receiving services from three CPS agencies, participated in this study. An example of significant positive growth across 18 assessment waves is shown for "support given to others" ($\beta_1 = 0.12$, $t = 4.22$, $p < .001$; see Table II.1). With multiwave data, a consistent estimate of the correlation of true initial status and true change can be obtained. The Tau correlation of -0.46 for these data indicates that teens who had limited supportive skills at entry tended to gain at a faster rate.

A significant decline was also found in negative attitudes and beliefs ($\beta_1 = -4.866$, $t = -2.249$, $p < .05$; see Table II.2). The estimated mean intercept, β_0, and mean growth rate, β_1, for attitudes and beliefs indicate that the average accumulated rating score for negative attitudes and beliefs was 76.832 at the beginning of group sessions, and the teens decreased an average score of 4.866 per session. The χ^2 for the intercept parameter suggests that participants varied significantly in their negative attitudes and beliefs at entry into the program, and the χ^2 for growth rate also suggests significant variation in the participants' acquisition of positive attitudes and beliefs. For attitudes and beliefs, the estimated reliabilities for initial status and growth rates were 0.57 and 0.49, respectively, indicating substantial signal in these data in terms of individual differences in both initial status and growth rates (such

Table II.1. Linear Model of Growth in Cofacilitator Ratings of Support to Others

Fixed Effect	Coefficient	SE	t Ratio	p Value
Mean initial status, β_0	2.30[a]	0.35	6.67	< .001
Mean growth rate, β_1	0.12	0.03	4.22	< .001

a. Behavior ratings on a 7-point scale ranging from 1 ("very low") to 7 ("very high").

Table II.2. Linear Model of Change (decline) in Negative Attitudes and Beliefs

Fixed Effect	Coefficient	SE	t Ratio	p Value
Mean initial status, β_0	76.832	6.434	11.941	< .001
Mean growth rate, β_1	−4.866	2.164	−2.249	< .05
Random Effect	Variance	df	χ^2	p Value
Initial status, r_0	659.130	27	62.590	< .001
Growth rate, r_1	64.434	27	53.094	< .01
Level-1 error	333.362			

reliability will increase with larger sample size and waves of data). Finally, the estimated correlation between true change and true initial status indicated that teens who had the most negative attitudes and beliefs at program entry tended to change at a faster rate. It can be inferred that this was a true negative relationship and not a spurious result of the measurement process.

Summary of Rationale and Preliminary Studies

Our model presumes that relationship violence begins with "initiation" behaviors prior to age 15 (e.g., teasing, pushing, throwing things) and escalates over the next several years of adolescence and young adulthood among those at risk. We have found support for this model on the basis of high school and CPS samples, indicating that both males and females engage in low-intensity coercion and abuse during midadolescence. Furthermore, youth with maltreatment backgrounds are more likely than nonmaltreated peers to be more coercive and abusive toward a dating partner (Wolfe, Wekerle, McEachran, et al., 1995). Finally, we have explored the nature and extent of "growth" or change in target behaviors among a pilot sample of CPS youths, indicating two primary findings: First, there is considerable evidence of growth occurring across the 18 weeks of the program, especially in terms of interest, support given and received, and similar issues. Second, pilot data from 28 subjects based on four assessment waves support the intervention approach in terms of revealing trends in the direction of positive growth in desired behaviors and decline in targeted behaviors.

PART

III

Program Sessions and Exercises

Program Sessions and Exercises

Introduction to the Youth Relationships Project Manual

To the readers of the Youth Relationships Project manual, welcome! We at the Youth Relationships Project have been very pleased with the enthusiasm that previous users of the manual (first edition, June 1994) have conveyed to us. We hope that you will find the following program manual both user-friendly and enjoyable.

This edition of the manual represents our most recent efforts to weave knowledge and awareness about violence, health promotion skills development, and social action toward ending violence into *each* of the 18 sessions in the program.

As a program aimed at preventing violence in intimate relationships, the program layout is intended to focus on key violence-related constructs, moving in coverage from the general (e.g., the role of anger in power and control issues) to the specific (e.g., individual's anger profiles). In examining violence in specific relationships, we first consider wife assault, later making the connections to dating violence as well as considering the social context of violence (sexism, patriarchy in institutions, and so on).

Overview of the Program Format

We start out examining what we consider to be the fundamental issue in relationship violence—the abuse of power. Power and control issues remain a continual theme throughout the 18 sessions, reemerging when we consider specific emotions such as anger, the different forms of violence in relationships, and media portrayals of men and women.

One of the ways young people come to understand healthy relationships is in the value of power sharing among partners and win-win solutions to problems. Rather than focusing solely on negative relationship styles, in each session there is an attempt to provide opportunities to explore the positive definition of healthy relationships, including assertive communication, empathy, providing positive feedback, and active listening, for example. The message that behavior is a choice—and therefore we are all responsible for our own behavior—is one that is critically examined by the teens throughout the program.

The final sessions are intended to maximize the youths' commitment to violence prevention by giving them the opportunity to initiate contact with social service agencies, experiencing positive interaction with key community programs. Finally, some form of social action initiative is undertaken by the youths, adding further to the young people's increasing feelings of success. We hope that, at the close of the program, the group celebration will be a tribute to the positive growth of the group, the individuals in the group, and the gains made on the issue of violence in close relationships.

Planning Note to Facilitators

Although some sessions require little more than a week's preparation time, others require fairly extensive advance preparation work by the cofacilitators, such as planning for speakers in Session 6. It is recommended that facilitators begin to make arrangements for the guest speakers as soon as possible. This is a sensitive issue that requires the support of local community agencies. Sessions 12 through 17 also require extensive community agency involvement and facilitators should contact these agencies in advance to request their participation and cooperation.

We suggest that as you read through the manual, you make special note of activities that require advance preparation. A "Notes" section has been included at the beginning of each session that can be used to assist in organizing and planning the sessions for current and future use.

There are six videos to be shown throughout the course of the program. Some will be available from your local library. The Resources section at the back of the manual provides information on where to purchase these videos.

Finally, some of the exercises in this manual are intended to be photocopied and handed out to the group participants.

SECTION

A

Violence in Close Relationships
It's All About Power

In addition to establishing a base for youth-centered group cohesion, the first three sessions set a conceptual framework for the entire group program. These sessions identify power dynamics as a fundamental concept that underscores many different forms of interpersonal violence: woman abuse, sexual assault, date rape, child abuse, racism, gay and lesbian bashing, and so on. To accomplish this goal, youths define power and violence and begin to examine the many diverse ways in which the abuse of power is expressed. In particular, the teens explore "control behavior" (i.e., behavior that is designed to elicit submission and obedience) such as explosive anger, threats to harm others, and attempts to isolate the victim from friends. Youths also begin to investigate alternatives to violence. They are given the opportunity to identify and explore their personal rights, and to identify and express their feelings positively and assertively.

Throughout the first three sessions, youths are also exposed to the fact that this program focuses specifically on men's violence toward women. Male and female adolescents have difficulty accepting the gender bias in interpersonal violence; that is, men are perpetrators of serious violence against women, and men's and women's expression of the same behavior cannot be compared as equal. Researchers of interpersonal violence note that although female partners may be violent, it is male violence that produces fear in the recipient. This is why men can use violence as a means of psychological and social control—it works. The youths are encouraged to critically examine the male role in interpersonal violence. The youths are also asked to think about violence as a "problem-solving strategy" and consider its effect on the relationship. It is emphasized that we choose our behavior, and violence is a behavior. The fact that not all men commit acts of interpersonal violence reinforces the choice aspect of this behavior. The teens are taught alternative skills to express their emotions and thoughts to increase their range of personal choice.

SESSION
1

Introduction to Group: Summary

GOALS	To establish a safe, comfortable, teen-centered environment for youths to identify attitudes and issues related to violence against women and to explore healthy relationships

SUMMARY OF OBJECTIVES	RESOURCES
I. Purpose of Program	Introductory Exercise
II. Introductory Exercise	Past participants
III. Overview: Past Participants	Flip chart and markers
IV. Group Agreement	Name tags
V. Questions	

NOTES: _____

_____

_____

_____

_____

_____

_____

_____

_____

Introduction to Group
Activity Plan

This program is about ending the abuse of power and control. It is essential that facilitators be aware of their behavior and role modeling from the outset, in their interactions with each other and the teenagers. Behaviors such as dominating the speaking floor, interrupting, or rushing in with "the" answer all send a message about who has more power. Power sharing and egalitarian relationships are among the most important goals of this program.

Cofacilitators'
Notes

The focus of the first session is getting to know one another and establishing a "safe container" in which to work. Name tags are not popular with teens, but ask them to go along with you for the first three meetings until participants learn each other's names. The teens will work together in this session to establish a group agreement, the terms of which they will each agree to adhere to for the course of the program.

TIME FRAME
(115 program minutes)

ACTIVITIES

(10 min)   I   Cofacilitators outline the purpose of the program.
                  The following four points should be emphasized:

                  1. When we are growing up, few people talk to us about what makes a relationship work, or what men and women want in a loving relationship. Therefore, we often get our information from television, videos, advertising, and

so on, and these sources often provide us with unhealthy role models.

2. The purpose of this program is to help young people dispel hurtful myths about gender roles and love relationships, to recognize and understand the abuse of power and control in relationships, and to talk about what makes a healthy relationship.

3. It is important that young people learn from one another in this program and talk about what they want and don't want in a relationship. We can also learn together about what we can do to prevent and stop violence in relationships, as individuals, as youths, and as members of a social community.

4. This is not counseling or group therapy; this is an educational program. It is an opportunity for the facilitators to learn about what works and what does not work in this violence prevention program, so the teens' feedback and ideas are really important.

(45 min)   II Introductory Ice-Breaker Exercise (see Session 1 exercises):

Cofacilitators should note that alternative ice-breakers are provided in this manual's Appendix A, and cofacilitators are free to use any other ice-breaker of their choice, including those that are not listed in the manual.

(10 min)   Break

(20 min)   III Past participants (ideally one male and one female) provide an overview of their experience in the program:

• What they learned

• What effect the program had on them

• What they enjoyed most about the program

• How they were feeling at their first session

• What feelings developed across the 18 sessions

Group members are given an opportunity to ask questions of the past participants.

If the program is new to the center that is sponsoring the group, or if old members are not available, this time slot can be replaced by asking the youth to share their experiences of other groups they have attended (*any* kind—not just counseling groups) or a discussion of what they imagine the group will be like.

(20 min)   IV Group members establish a group agreement:

The group brainstorms the "rules" for the group agreement. These "rules" are noted on a flip chart and posted for the duration of the group. Group members are told that they will be asked to sign the group agreement in Session 3 as a sign of their continuing commitment to the group and to the group agreement.

Facilitators may introduce the exercise by stating that although this is an educational group, some people may choose to talk about things that are personal and that they wish only the group to know. Group rules are a way of making it safe for people to talk about their experiences and to share their ideas, and a way of ensuring that everyone is treated with respect.

Because this is the teens' group, ask them what kinds of group rules they would like to have. The following are examples of some of the rules youths may wish to implement:

- Confidentiality
- No put-downs
- Honesty
- No smoking inside
- Start and end on time
- Attend regularly
- One person speaks at a time

It is particularly important that the "rules" are generated by the teenagers and not by the cofacilitators. Emphasize to the teens that this is "their" group and it is important for *them* to establish the group agreement. It is also important to emphasize that each teen is personally responsible for sticking to the agreement.

Notably, there is a strong possibility that participants will disclose a number of past and present experiences with violence and abuse as they become more comfortable with the group. At this time, cofacilitators should inform the youths that there are limits to confidentiality and that facilitators have a legal responsibility to report disclosures of current violence to their social workers.

(10 min)   V   Introduce the idea of a "Parking Lot"—a space set aside on a chalkboard or on a piece of flip chart paper where topics or issues not covered by the program, but of interest to the youths, can be noted to come back to when there is time.

EXERCISES

Ice-Breaker Exercise
Complete the Sentence—Biographies

The statements below are each placed on individual cards and one card is given to each participant, including the facilitators. Number off participants: one, two, one, two . . . Instruct the youths that "ones" will remain at their places while "twos" move to the next open seat to the right after each statement. Each participant turns to his or her partner and asks the partner to complete the sentence on his or her card. The answers as well as anything else about them that comes up to share with the group should be recorded on the card. At a signal from a facilitator, the "two" moves to the next partner. Once back to their original seats, the facilitator asks who would like to be introduced first. Once a person volunteers, others are asked to explain which statement they read and what they learned about the person. Not all participants meet one another. After all participants who spoke to this person have shared their knowledge, this person is asked if she or he has anything to add or clarify.

Statement Cards

1. My favorite restaurant is _____ because . . .
2. If I were given a million dollars today, I would _____ because . . .
3. My favorite animal is _____ because . . .
4. The best day of the week for me is _____ because . . .
5. My favorite musical group or television show is _____ because . . .
6. My favorite place in the world is _____ because . . .
7. In my spare time, the three things I like to do most are . . .
8. As a child, my idol/hero was _____ because . . .
9. My favorite game is _____ because . . .
10. The thing that I do best is _____.
11. My favorite elementary/secondary school teacher was _____ because . . .
12. If I had to spend a year on a deserted island, the two things I would take with me are . . .

Notes on People I Met . . .

_____

Name:
Question:

Answers:

_____

Name:
Question:

Answers:

_____

Name:
Question:

Answers:

_____

Name:
Question:

Answers:

_____

SESSION
2

Power in Relationships: Explosions and Assertions

GOALS

To recognize the roots of violence as the abuse of power and control and to begin to examine anger as one potential form of abuse of power

---

SUMMARY OF OBJECTIVES

I. Check-in
II. Recap
III. Exploring Social Power
IV. Exploring Anger
V. Choices and Responsibility
VI. Defining Assertiveness

RESOURCES

Name tags
Flip chart and markers
Stand-Up Exercise
Power Relationships Exercise
Three Chair Exercise

NOTES: _____

_____

_____

_____

_____

_____

_____

SESSION
2

$$ \textit{Power in Relationships} $$
Activity Plan

*Cofacilitators'
Notes*

Often, the second session has a few new members joining who were not able to attend Session 1. Adding to the group agreement what new members believe to be important welcomes and values their involvement.

In this and in many of the upcoming sessions, the youths will be asked to "brainstorm"—to come up with ideas individually or as a group for a particular problem or issue. It is helpful if cofacilitators list their ideas on a piece of flip chart paper and post the lists on the wall.

In this session, we will be exploring social power. There are many social relationships with power imbalances that leave people in a "one-up" or "one-down" position. The concepts *one-up* and *one-down* refer to the social power one person has in relation to another; that is, a teacher has more social power than a student. The student would be considered to be in the one-down position and the teacher would be considered to be in the one-up position.

TIME FRAME
(120 program minutes)

ACTIVITIES

(15 min)

I Check in. Introduce the notion of a check-in. Check-ins take place at the start of each meeting to allow everyone a chance to know what kind of week we each had and what mood we are in at the start of group. Participants may check in with a feeling word (important rehearsal for assertive communication) and also a high and/or low point of their week. In the following sessions, the teens can lead check-in. For example,

44

one youth could be chosen to lead the entire check-in exercise. Alternatively, either a cofacilitator or a youth can start the check-in and then choose the next person to check in, asking him or her to indicate how he or she is feeling and to share the high and/or low point of his or her week. After checking in, this person would then choose the next person to check in, and so on.

Note: Check-ins provide an effective vehicle to promote group relationship development and group cohesion. Often, sharing of personal information provides the most powerful material for that session. Cofacilitators should be careful of time constraints, however; check-ins can easily take half the session if not guided along!

(10 min)   II   Recap: Introduce the notion of a "recap," which will follow the check-in at each session. Recaps provide a very brief review of what was covered during the previous session. The purpose of the recap is to facilitate learning and to update any youths who may have been absent from the previous session. Initially, the cofacilitators should prompt the youths to recall what was discussed or learned in the previous session. Eventually, the teens themselves can lead the recap, perhaps with a different youth being chosen each week to lead the recap.

(10 min)   III   Exploring Social Power: Introduce the following set of exercises by telling the youths that one focus of the group is power and how the abuse of power is connected to violence.

(10 min)   (a) Brainstorm: "What is power" (or what makes a person powerful)?

- *Power:* There are many definitions of power and it may be difficult to define (Babcock, Waltz, Jacobson, & Gottman, 1993).

Essentially, there are three elements to power:

- *Power bases*—personal assets and resources such as knowledge and skills that form the basis of one partner's control over another
- *Power processes*—interactional techniques, such as assertiveness, aggressiveness, persuasion, problem solving, that an individual uses in an attempt to gain control
- *Power outcomes*—who makes the final decision, who wins the situation

If not suggested by the teens, include in the definition that power is also access to resources, jobs, education, protection under the law, representation in government, and so on.

(10 min)   (b) The Stand-Up Exercise illustrates the effects of social labels that place certain groups in a one-down position (see Session 2 exercises).

(15 min)   (c) The Power Relationships Exercise compares those who have social power and those who do not. To conduct this exercise, use the Power Chart and point out that the focus for this program is on power relationships between men and women (see Session 2 exercises).

Note: As part of the discussion on power groups and non-power groups, cofacilitators should acknowledge their own power and privilege (e.g., adult, facilitator, white, male). This role models for teens the importance of acknowledging and taking responsibility for social power. During this exercise, it is also important to distinguish social power from personal power. Personal power stems from things that we as individuals are particularly good at, such as sports, music. Personal power is not dependent on social power.

(10 min)   Break

(15 min)   IV Exploring Anger and Its Connection to Power: Explain to the youths that anger and violence often go hand in hand. Angry people are often perceived to be very powerful, and anger can be used to intimidate or make people feel powerless if it is not expressed in a healthy way. The rest of the session focuses on what it means to be angry and how we handle our own and other people's anger.

Explore an argument scenario. This may be taken from a recent experience of the youths or facilitators, or may be made up by the facilitators prior to the session. This exercise helps further our understanding of what happens when we get angry, what other feelings are present, and how our attitudes influence our response. Discussion questions should include the following:

   • What might the angry person(s) be thinking? feeling?

   • What values, attitudes, or beliefs are underlying these thoughts/feelings?

   • Do these relate to the power imbalances discussed previously?

   • If each person involved had a better understanding of the thoughts and feelings of the other, would this have changed the outcome of the argument?

   • Who is responsible for actions taken?

(15 min)   V Choices and Responsibility: Present the notion that no one can "make" us behave in a certain way if we become angry with

them (i.e., someone is not raising my hand for me to hit another). Discuss the idea that it is OK to feel angry; it is what we do with that anger that is sometimes not OK. Regardless of the situation, we have a range of responsible choices.

Brainstorm what these choices are and discuss which choices are OK (nonviolent/nonabusive) and which are not OK (violent or abusive). The list of choices should include the following:

- Discuss issue calmly

- Yell and scream

- Leave and figure out our feelings and how we wish to respond

- Hit the other person

- Hit/punch/kick something (a wall, table, and so on)

- Put the other person down

Emphasize that we are responsible for the way we choose to respond. Our behavior is our choice. Also emphasize that we are *not* responsible for someone who chooses to react to their anger with violence. If you are the victim of someone else's violence, *you are not to blame.*

(20 min)   VI   Defining Assertiveness: Introduce this exercise by stating that conflict and disagreement are a common part of love relationships. However, in the same way that people don't talk to teenagers about what makes a healthy relationship, people rarely talk to us about how to "fight fair." Explain that the following exercise demonstrates three different ways of handling conflict (passively, aggressively, and assertively).

Three Chair Exercise (see Session 2 exercises): This exercise provides a concrete definition of assertive behavior by comparing it with passive and aggressive behavior. It also provides an illustration of how we can handle conflict in a way that is respectful to ourselves and to other people. After the exercise has been completed, discuss how being assertive ensures that we are respecting our right to be treated fairly and the right of others to be treated fairly, and why it's important to respect this right when asserting ourselves.

EXERCISES

Stand-Up Exercise: Nonpower Groups

Facilitator

1. This exercise helps us think about how it feels to be in a nonpower group. I'm going to read a number of statements that show how society labels people and places us in a one-down position (this does not mean we each do not have personal power; we do!). If the statement fits you, please *silently* stand up for a few moments and notice:

   • Who is with you
   • Who is not with you
   • How you're feeling during the exercise

2. You *do not* have to identify yourself as a member of a group that is called out if you don't want to, but notice feelings about *not* identifying! If you are unsure about whether or not you belong to a certain group, you decide what makes most sense for you.

3. *"Please stand if _____."*

   (Read list of "labeling statements" that follows. Allow a few moments to stand between statements.) Following the first statement, and reminding again every so often, make the following comment:

   "Notice who is standing with you; notice who is not. Notice how you are feeling. OK, you may sit down."

The Labeling Statements

1. If you are a woman.
2. If you are a person of color and/or born in another country.
3. If you are Native Canadian/American.
4. If you are under 18 years of age.
5. If you were raised by a single parent or currently are a single parent.
6. If you come from a family with little money.
7. If you were raised in the country, rurally.
8. If you were ever held back a grade in school or pushed toward a trade you did not want to do.
9. If you have a visible or nonvisible disability.

10. If you come from a family where alcohol or drugs were/are a problem.

11. If you are lesbian, gay, or bisexual (and/or someone in your family or a close friend is gay/lesbian/bisexual).

12. If you grew up with violence in your household.

13. If as a child you ever had an adult's needs put ahead of yours.

Process Questions

- How did people feel during the exercise? (i.e., vulnerable, shy, embarrassed)

- How did it feel being separate from the group? (i.e., put on the spot)

It is helpful to reinforce that these categories are labels put on people that often put them in a nonpower, or one-down, position in our society.

(SOURCE: From *Teens Need Teens: A Manual for Adults Helping Teens Stop Violence*, Creighton & Kivel, 1990. Adapted with permission.)

Power Chart/Oppression

1. The Power Chart is taped onto chalkboard/wall and the power relationships are read aloud.

POWER CHART

Power	*Nonpower*
Men	Women
White	People of Color
Adult	Child/Youth
Adult	Elder
Rich	Poor
Heterosexual	Gay/Lesbian/Bisexual
Able-bodied	Disabled
Boss	Worker
Teacher	Student

2. Comment:

- The Power Chart shows some of the inequities of power that exist in our culture. The power group is allowed to have social power while the nonpower group is not. The Power Chart shows the power imbalances in relationships that create the environment for abuse to take place.

• Again, this does not mean the nonpower group does not have personal power. What it means is that our society has *labeled them* and placed them in a one-down position. Often the nonpower groups experience violence, usually at the hands of the corresponding power group.

3. Questions:

• Which of the different non-power groups did we see in the Stand-Up Exercise?

• What are the different kinds of violence that happen to the nonpower groups, usually at the hands of the corresponding power groups? (e.g., What kinds of violence are done to kids by adults? to people of color by white people? to women by men?)

Attached to the Power Chart, draw a third column. List the kinds of violence that happen to the nonpower groups at the hands of the corresponding power groups. Once a list is compiled, write the word *Oppression* in the heading and note that this is what we call these forms of abuse.

Power	Nonpower	Oppression
Men	Women	hitting, neglect,
White	People of Color	exploitation, verbal
Adult	Child/Youth	abuse, physical abuse,
Adult	Elder	withheld rights and
Rich	Poor	choices, rape, harass-
Heterosexual	Gay/Lesbian/Bisexual	ment, poverty, poor
Able-bodied	Disabled	care, economic abuse,
Boss	Worker	segregation, brutality
Teacher	Student	

4. Summary Comments

We all experience *both sides* of the chart at some time in our lives. We all know what it's like to have someone have *power over us.* This is what woman abuse is all about.

It is also important to note that some people face multiple barriers and are at higher risk of being abused if they face numerous nonpower social labels (e.g., disabled Native girl).

The *purpose of violence* is to keep people in their places.

We are all born with no knowledge of prejudice, but we learn to categorize and accept categories (internalized oppression). A child is not born with the knowledge of racial slurs, or an innate hate for homosexuals, for example. This is all learned.

But how do we learn this prejudice, and do we go along with it if it hurts someone (including ourselves and our own relationships)?

Assertiveness Training: Three Chair Exercise

Materials

    3 empty chairs
    chalkboard or flip chart
    cofacilitator recording

Procedure

1. Set out three empty chairs and inform participants that the "actor" facilitator will act differently sitting in each chair:

   In chair 1, facilitator will act passively
   In chair 2, aggressively
   In chair 3, assertively

2. The cofacilitator (recorder) draws a behavior/feelings grid on the chalkboard or flip chart.

	Passive	*Aggressive*	*Assertive*
Behavior			
Feelings			

3. The group members are asked to indicate which behaviors and feelings they observed for each category. As the actor moves from chair to chair—from passive to aggressive to assertive—the recorder notes the behaviors (body language, voice tone, eye contact, and so on) in each chair. The actor returns to chair 1 and repeats the performance, this time looking for the feelings a person behaving in this way may have. The recorder also notes these on the grid.

Example

	Passive	*Aggressive*	*Assertive*
Behavior	quiet no eye contact fidgety	standing up clenched fist yelling	good posture even voice calm
Feelings	bad about self walked over afraid	fear, bad powerful embarrassed afterward	true to self nervous good about self

The actor will ask prompting questions in the mode of the chair in which she or he is sitting. For example:

Passive Chair *Behaviors:*

- "When I am in this chair (soft voice, hunched, and averting eyes), what do you notice about my behavior and body language?"

- "If I was upset with you—I'm not, you're great—but if I was, I would . . ., well maybe . . ., no forget it." (Participants continue to yell out descriptions and recorder may assist with prompts about how actor is doing with telling you what she or he is upset about.)

Feelings:

- "What might I be feeling in this chair? How might I be feeling about myself? Anything else?"

Aggressive Chair *Behaviors:*

- "In this chair, how can you tell I'm aggressive? (yelling) What do you mean my voice! What about my voice! (Stands and towers over someone.) What do you know anyway, you're just a butt head . . ."

Feelings:

- "What do you think I'm feeling in this chair" (still in aggressive mode with raised voice and so on): OK, bad about myself. What else? How might I feel afterward?"

Assertive Chair *Behaviors:*

- "In this chair I am sitting straight, chin up, making eye contact with you and speaking with a calm voice.

Feelings:

- "What do you think I'm feeling in this chair?" (spoken calmly, assuredly, continuing to make eye contact)

4. "Recorder" facilitator briefly summarizes the chart and the differences between assertive and nonassertive behaviors, and also discusses the benefits seen in acting assertively (reasonable, less likely to be dismissed as passive or aggressive, and so on).

SESSION
3

Defining Relationship Violence: Power Abuses

| GOALS | To define woman abuse and clarify myths |
| | To define violence and explore different forms of violence and to explore assertiveness |

SUMMARY OF OBJECTIVES

RESOURCES

I. Check-in
II. Recap
III. Myths and Facts of
    Woman Abuse
IV. Define Violence
V. Personal Rights
VI. Personal Inventories
VII. Identify Feelings

Myths and Facts Questionnaire
Power and Control Wheel
Personal rights handout
Sentence Completion Exercise
Feelings handout
Identifying Feelings Exercise
With and Without Words Exercise

NOTES: _____

_____

_____

_____

_____

_____

_____

_____

SESSION
3

![horizontal bar]

Defining Relationship Violence
Activity Plan

Cofacilitators'
Notes

This session begins to explore the question: "What is violence?" Different forms of violence are discussed and cofacilitators emphasize that this program focuses on woman abuse that occurs in intimate relationships—in dating relationships, in marriages, *and* in intimate teen relationships. With this session there also begins a shift in focus from the general to the personal level. The youths are encouraged to consider what their personal rights are and to develop "personal inventories" that explore what we do, think, and feel when we are angry. Although teens are given the opportunity to share their personal experiences and insights with the group, at this point in time there may only be a few who are comfortable with this. It is important to respect the needs of those who are not yet ready to volunteer personal information or insights. This session also asks youths to do activities that involve reading. Cofacilitators should be sensitive to the fact that some may not have sophisticated reading skills and offer assistance where needed.

For some exercises, it is suggested that you have youths work in pairs. This format helps develop comfortable relationships and over time fosters better group cohesion, because the teens get to know each other and because the quieter teens get an opportunity to speak up. It is best if the facilitators assign pairs to ensure that the same two youths do not always work together (which may form destructive cliques within the group) and to ensure that those who do not know each other very well get an opportunity to work together and establish a relationship.

At some point during this session, participants (youths and cofacilitators) are asked to sign the group agreement that was established in the first session.

TIME FRAME	ACTIVITIES

(120 program minutes)

(10 min)   I   Check in.

(10 min)   II   Recap.

(25 min)   III   Myths and Facts of Woman Abuse Questionnaire: Ask youths to take 10 minutes to complete the Myths and Facts Questionnaire (see Session 3 exercises for questionnaire and answers). This exercise can be completed individually or in pairs. After 10 minutes, go over the correct responses to the questionnaire with them. Facilitators may want to make note of relative strengths and weaknesses regarding the teens' knowledge of violence and abuse.

(15 min)   IV   Brainstorm: What is violence (e.g., Is it violence if I yell where nobody can hear me?), and why do people use violence? Summarize with the following definition: *Violence is any attempt to control or dominate another person.*

                Distribute the Power and Control Wheel (see Session 3 exercises) and discuss the various forms of violence that are often a part of woman abuse.

(10 min)   Break

(15 min)   V   Personal Rights: Introduce this exercise by stating that it often seems harder to be assertive and respectful of our rights when having a conflict with someone who has more power than we do (e.g., when a teen is having a conflict with an adult).

                Brainstorm: Why is it sometimes hard to be assertive? (e.g., We don't want to hurt someone, be afraid to make mistakes, or have someone mad at us). Although it is sometimes difficult, being direct with others helps us to understand each other better, even if it creates a conflict. We also have a right to express our feelings (in a respectful manner), no matter what the circumstances. We may not always get what we want, but we always have the right to ask. We also have many personal rights that we often take for granted and many personal rights that we don't allow ourselves.

                Review the handout: Your Personal Rights (see Session 3 exercises). *Note that we should remember that other people also have these same rights.*

(15 min)   VI   Personal Inventories: Participants take a few minutes to complete the personal inventory Sentence Completion exercise

(see Session 3 exercises). Participants are asked to share their responses if they wish. Be sure that participants differentiate between what they were *thinking* and what they were *feeling*. We often have a hard time identifying all of our feelings when we are angry (e.g., we may also be feeling hurt, embarrassed, rejected, lonely). Also, try to summarize whether most participants had positive or negative feelings about their conflict resolution strategies. Indicate that one focus of the group will be on developing conflict resolution strategies so that conflicts will have more satisfactory outcomes. Use any difficulties the youths may have had in identifying feelings as a springboard for the next exercise.

(20 min)   VII Identifying Feelings: Explain to the teens that although we are all fairly good at identifying feelings of happiness and anger, most of us have a hard time identifying more subtle or less obvious feelings. Our ability to identify these feelings is important because it is often the underlying feelings that lead to the dominant feelings of anger and happiness. Two exercises are used to help youths better identify their feelings and to increase their repertoire of labels for their feelings.

Distribute the Feelings handout (see Session 3 exercises) to assist them with the next two exercises. Allow the teens approximately 10 minutes to complete the Identify the Feeling exercise and the With and Without Words exercise (see Session 3 exercises). Both exercises work well in pairs. After 10 minutes, take up the responses to both exercises with the participants.

EXERCISES

Myths and Facts of Woman Abuse Questionnaire

Please take 10 minutes to complete this quiz. Please do *not* put your name anywhere on the quiz.

In items 1 to 4, please mark the appropriate answer A, B, C, D, E, or F.

1. What proportion of Canadian women are assaulted by the man they live with?
   A. 1 out of 100
   B. 1 out of 75
   C. 1 out of 50
   D. 1 out of 20
   E. 1 out of 7

2. What percentage of family violence is directed at women and children?

50%	60%	70%	80%	90%	95%
A	B	C	D	E	F

3. Which of the following statements is true?
   A. Women are *much more* likely to be assaulted by *their partner* than by a stranger on the street.
   B. Women are *somewhat more* likely to be assaulted by *their partner* than by a stranger on the street.
   C. Women are *just as likely* to be assaulted by *their partner* as they are by a stranger on the street.
   D. Women are *somewhat more* likely to be assaulted *by a stranger* than by their partner.
   E. Women are *much more* likely to be assaulted by a *stranger* than by their partner.

4. Which of the following statements is accurate (true)?
   A. In cases of wife assault, the police can only file charges if the woman wants them to.
   B. A woman needs a witness in order to press assault charges against her spouse.
   C. Assault against one's spouse carries a lighter maximum sentence than does an assault on a stranger.
   D. The criminal code of Canada treats wife assault the same as stranger assault.
   E. Charges will not be filed in cases of wife assault unless the woman requires medical attention due to the assault.

In this next section (items 5 to 17), we would like your opinion on each of the statements. For each statement, please mark A, B,

C, D, or E in accordance with the following scale:

Strongly Agree	Agree	Undecided	Disagree	Disagree Strongly
A	**B**	**C**	**D**	**E**

5. Assaulted women could just leave their partner if they really wanted to.

6. Some women deserve the violence that they experience.

7. Poverty causes family violence.

8. Alcohol causes family violence.

9. As long as children are not abused, they are not affected by witnessing violence in the home.

10. Violence is a private family matter.

11. The community has no right to intervene in family violence.

12. If someone is abusive in a dating relationship, he or she will stop when married.

13. A violent fight can "clear the air," it probably will not happen again.

14. When a man abuses a woman, he tries to control her.

15. When a husband and wife share equal power in a marriage, it is bound to cause some violent fights.

16. If someone swears at or intimidates another person, this is abuse.

17. Schools should have a role in increasing awareness of the effects of violence and how to prevent it.

(SOURCE: Based on information from Gelles & Straus, 1988; Sinclair, 1985.)

Answers to Questions

1. What proportion of Canadian women are assaulted by the man they live with?

   E. 1 out of 7

2. What percentage of family violence is directed at women and children?

   F. 95%

3. The following statement is true.

   A. Women are *much more* likely to be assaulted by *their partner* than by a stranger on the street.

      Women are 13 times more likely to be assaulted by their partner in London, Ontario, than by a stranger on the street (London Family Court Clinic).

4. The following statement is accurate:

   D. The criminal code of Canada treats wife assault the same as stranger assault.

(SOURCE: From Jaffe, Suderman, Reitzel, and Killop, 1993. Used with permission.)

Myths and Facts About Woman Abuse

MYTH: Woman abuse is not a major criminal and social problem.

FACTS:
- One in seven women are abused by their partner.
- Two women per week, in Canada, are killed by their partner.
- In the United States, there are more than twice as many women injured as a result of domestic violence than there are women injured due to rapes, homicides, and muggings combined.

MYTH: Assaulted women could just leave their partner if they really wanted to.

FACTS:
- There are major financial, emotional, and social barriers to separation. The three best predictors of women staying are economic dependence, poor self-concept, and witnessing violence in the family of origin.
- The characteristics of battered women tend to keep them as prisoners in their own home (e.g., isolation, sense of helplessness, hope for change in the abuser, minimizing the abuse, blaming themselves, ambivalence).

MYTH: Men who beat their wives share the following characteristics: lower socioeconomic status, alcohol or drug abuse, and mental illness.

FACTS:
- Woman abuse crosses all socioeconomic strata.
- Although drugs or alcohol can make a violent episode worse, they are not the cause of the violence. Alcohol and drugs are used by batterers as an excuse for abusive behavior.
- The best predictor of a batterer is witnessing violence in the family of origin; 75% of men who abuse their wives witnessed violence when they were children.

MYTH: Woman abuse is a private family matter that family members can resolve on their own without community involvement.

FACTS:
- Woman abuse is a crime, punishable under the *Criminal Code of Canada.*
- Most homicides and aggravated assaults are preceded by calls for community assistance: 90% of homicides have at least one prior police call for assistance; 50% of homicides have *five or more* prior police calls.

- Children exposed to wife battering often have a level of adjustment problems comparable to that of children who are physically abused themselves.
- Woman abuse is strongly associated with delinquency (young offenders) and adult criminality.

MYTH: Women provoke or deserve the violence.

FACTS: No one deserves to be beaten, no matter what kind of person they are. Provocation is an excuse the offender uses to avoid responsibility for his own behavior.

(SOURCE: Based on information from Gelles & Straus, 1988; Sinclair, 1985; Statistics Canada, 1993.)

Your Personal Rights

1. The right to act in ways that promote your dignity and self-respect as long as others' rights are not violated in the process.
2. The right to be treated with respect.
3. The right to say "No," without feeling guilty.
4. The right to experience and express your feelings.
5. The right to take time to slow down and think.
6. The right to change your mind.
7. The right to *ask* for what you want.
8. The right to do less than you are humanly capable of doing.
9. The right to ask for information.
10. The right to make MISTAKES and accept responsibility.
11. The right to feel good about yourself.

(SOURCE: Compiled from Smith, 1975)

Sentence Completion

1. The last thing that made me so angry that I felt I would blow up was:

   _____

   _____

   _____

2. The things I thought about at that time were:

   _____

   _____

   _____

3. The feelings I had at that time were:

   _____

   _____

   _____

4. What I did:

   _____

   _____

   _____

5. Afterward, I felt:

   _____

   _____

   _____

With and Without Words

1. Nancy, who had been talking a lot in the group, suddenly became silent. Describe two feelings that might have caused Nancy to do this.

   A. _____

   B. _____

2. Without expression, Lucy suddenly changed the subject of the group's discussion. What are two different feelings that might have been responsible for Lucy's changing the subject?

   A. _____

   B. _____

3. Whenever George made a comment in the group, he watched the leader's face. What are two different feelings that might have led George to watch the leader so intently?

   A. _____

   B. _____

4. While the group discussion was going on, Betty became more and more tense and restless. Finally, she got up abruptly and left the room without saying a word. Describe two feelings that might have caused Betty to leave.

   A. _____

   B. _____

5. Ron was seriously describing a fight he and a friend had earlier. In the middle of his discussion, John began to laugh. Describe two different feelings that might have caused John to laugh.

   A. _____

   B. _____

Feelings

HELPFUL	ABSORBED	STRONG
KIND	LOVING	THANKFUL
SAD	DEPRESSED	DISCOURAGED
EMBARRASSED	HUMILIATED	JEALOUS
PUT DOWN	SUSPICIOUS	INTERESTED
AFRAID	TENSE	WORRIED
HAPPY	ELATED	PEACEFUL
RELAXED	PROUD	CURIOUS
FRIENDLY	VIGOROUS	CONFIDENT
TORN	HURT	FRUSTRATED
EXCITED	WEAK	DEFEATED
SHY	BELITTLED	CONFUSED
SURPRISED	ASTONISHED	LONELY
FORGOTTEN	LEFT OUT	ANGRY
HOSTILE	ENRAGED	IRRITATED
DISPLEASED	FUMING	MAD
RESENTFUL	ASHAMED	GUILTY
PLAYFUL	JOKING	WITTY
MISERABLE	TROUBLED	

Figure 3.1. Power and Control Wheel

SOURCE: Domestic Abuse Intervention Project, 206 West Fourth Street, Duluth, MN 55806, (218) 722-4134. Used with permission.

Breaking the Cycle
of Violence
What We Can Choose to Do and
What We Can Choose Not to Do

The next three sessions build on the previous three sessions by continuing to examine power dynamics in relationships. The teens will reflect on how a person breaks out of a cycle of violence, a cycle that may span generations. These issues become both intimate and interactive with viewing the *Break the Cycle* video in Session 5 and the presentations of speakers in Session 6 (a survivor of woman abuse and a former batterer). These "real-life" testimonies about intimate violence enable the youths to ask questions about violence and recognize the power and control issues they have examined.

An important component of this section is the rehearsal of nonviolent relationship skills. Positive communication is the main focus, including specific skills: active listening, empathy, and emotional expressiveness. A strategy for approaching interpersonal problems (DESC: describe, express, specify, consequences; Bower & Bower, 1976) is introduced and used throughout the remainder of the group. Specific communication skills are enhanced: the need for males to ensure consent in sexual relations and the value of females being clear, up-front, and safe.

Ultimately, at the close of Section B, it is hoped that teens can recognize and label the various forms of interpersonal violence, understanding their power dynamics. Furthermore, the goal is for youths to gain in their ability to express their feelings, opinions, and behaviors based on the values of equality, respect, and sharing of power, and to solve problems with a nonviolent win-win outcome.

SESSION
4

Defining Powerful Relationships: Equality, Empathy, and Emotional Expressiveness

GOALS

To define different aspects of healthy relationships
To compare and contrast healthy and unhealthy relationships
To develop healthy relationship skills

SUMMARY OF OBJECTIVES

I. Check-in
II. Recap
III. Define Healthy
Relationships
IV. Attending Exercise
V. Define Empathy
VI. Communicating
Effectively

RESOURCES

Attending Exercise
Empathy Exercise
Picture Drawing Exercise
Rumor Mill Exercise

NOTES: _____

_____

_____

_____

_____

_____

SESSION
4

Defining Powerful Relationships
Activity Plan

Cofacilitators'
Notes

Thus far, much of the focus has been on defining violence, power imbalances, and other aspects of unhealthy relationships (i.e., the unhealthy expression of anger and the inability to express feelings). This session focuses on defining healthy relationships and developing skills that can contribute to the development of healthy, nonviolent relationships.

TIME FRAME
(115 program minutes)

ACTIVITIES

(10 min)   I   Check in.

(10 min)   II Recap.

(15 min)   III Introduction to Defining Healthy Relationships: Introduce today's session by explaining that the session will focus on our understanding and development of skills that help create healthy, nonviolent relationships. These skills will include active listening (i.e., paraphrasing, empathy, and asking for clarification) and learning to identify internal and external cues that signify emotions.

Ask youths to brainstorm what they think a healthy relationship looks like. If they do not come up with the ideas contained in the following list, suggest these qualities and ask for the teens' opinions:

• Trust

- Sharing of thoughts, ideas, feelings

- Respect for each other's thoughts, ideas, and feelings

- Encouraging and supporting each other to grow

- Each person feels loved and valued

- Each person feels safe to express disagreement and negative feelings including anger, disappointment, frustration, and so on

- Each person feels safe when the other person expresses disagreement and negative feelings

Defining Unhealthy Relationships: Once the list has been completed, ask youths to identify the opposite qualities; for example, the opposite of trust might be jealousy. Ask the teens to identify why these qualities are unhealthy.

(20 min)   IV   Attending Exercise (see Session 4 exercises): This exercise demonstrates what good attending and nonattending look like. Following the completion of this exercise, discuss how rushing in with advice or solutions is another example of nonattending behavior because of the following:

- Partner may not be ready to make any decisions.

- Partner may only need someone to listen, not to give answers.

- Rushing in with advice implies that the partner's feelings are unimportant.

- Partner may feel like you think he or she isn't capable of making his or her own decisions.

(10 min)   Break

(15 min)   V   Empathy: Ask the participants to define empathy. Summarize the discussion by providing the following working definition: *Empathy is the ability to put yourself in someone else's shoes and see how the world feels from his or her point of view.* Point out the emphasis on understanding another person's *feelings.*

Empathy Exercise (see Session 4 exercises).

(30 min)   VI   Communicating Effectively: The following exercises are implemented as a means of discovering how communication can be misunderstood.

Seeking clarification: Picture Drawing Exercise (see Session 4 exercises).

Paraphrasing: Rumor Mill Exercise (see Session 4 exercises).

(10 min)   VII   Recognizing Internal and External Cues for Emotion: Begin this exercise by defining internal cues (signs that only you can notice

that indicate you are starting to feel angry, sad, nervous, or the like) and external cues (signs that someone else is feeling, for example, nervous, even if she or he doesn't say anything). Brainstorm two separate lists for internal and external cues. Start by suggesting a particular emotion and asking the teens to provide an example of an internal and an external sign for that emotion, such as feelings of anger and/or feelings of fear. Summarize this exercise by stating that learning to recognize our own internal cues for emotion helps us better decide how we want to express that emotion, and that learning to recognize external cues helps us to better understand where other people are coming from.

EXERCISES

Empathy Exercise

Divide the youths into pairs and assign one youth to the role of the listener and the other to the role of the speaker. One cofacilitator outlines the task for the speakers, and the other outlines the task for the listeners. Neither group should know what the other group is doing ahead of time. Once the teens understand their roles, have them sit with their partners and provide them with 2 minutes to conduct the exercise.

Speaker Role: Provide the speakers with "problem scenarios." (One scenario can be used for all the pairs, or if the youths seem ready, ask the speakers to use a real problem that they would be willing to discuss with the listener.) *Do not tell the listener what the problem is ahead of time.*

Problem Example: You have just begun working in the local convenience store. A few weeks after you started, money began to be missing from the till, and the manager accused you of stealing it, even though the manager had no proof. You have absolutely nothing to do with the missing money and you know the accusation is unfair. You really need the job, but the manager has threatened to fire you the next time money is missing.

Listener Role: Present the listener's role by stating that they are going to "play detective." Their only job is to try and understand the speaker's underlying feelings. In this exercise, the listener listens to the speaker describe the problem and responds *only by reflecting back the speaker's feelings.* For example, they can respond by saying, "It sounds like you feel really angry," or "it seems like you're really hurt that the manager would think that." Tell the listeners not to ask any questions; their only job is to try and understand and reflect back the speakers' feelings. Warn them that this will probably feel strange and a little awkward but that we will only give the pairs 2 minutes to do the exercise.

Note: This is a real challenge for the listeners! It will probably help to give them the Feelings handout from last week to use as a guide for this exercise.

Group Discussion: Once the youths have gathered back together, ask the listeners how they felt during the exercise. They will probably say that it felt awkward and artificial. Next, ask the speakers how it felt to be listened to in this manner, and how it felt to have their feelings reflected back to them. In general, the speakers will probably have more positive things to say about the experience. Compare and contrast the listeners' and the speakers' experience of the exercise. Summarize by saying that new ways of communicating can feel really strange at first, especially because we're often taught that we should handle another person's problems by providing answers. However, this is rarely helpful to the person with the problem, and often not what he or she is looking for. Finish by saying that empathy is about really trying to understand the other person's position rather than simply trying to win an argument (sometimes people even forget what they are arguing about).

Picture Drawing Exercise

Divide the teens into pairs and have them sit with their backs to one another. Make sure one member of each pair can see a piece of paper that you will post on the wall, and make sure that the other member of the pair *cannot* see this piece of paper. The person who cannot see the piece of paper needs a pencil and a piece of drawing paper.

Once the pairs are arranged, post a piece of flip chart paper on the wall. On this paper, draw a simple picture of a common object (e.g., a skeleton key or a house). The person who can see this design must tell his or her partner how to draw it. *The person doing the drawing is not allowed to say anything or ask any questions.* Give the pairs 2 minutes to complete the drawing.

Once the 2 minutes have passed, the pairs can compare their drawing to the one on the wall. Summarize this exercise by asking the drawers how their drawings might have been more accurate if they had been allowed to ask questions. Ask the persons giving directions if it would have been easier if they could have checked out the accuracy of their directions. Finally, point out that communication is a lot more effective when we don't make assumptions and when we can ask for clarification.

Rumor Mill Exercise

Send all the youths out of the room except for one. Tell this youth the story as outlined below. Then bring in the next youth and have the first youth relay the story as accurately as possible. Then bring in the third youth and have the second youth relay the story as accurately as possible. Continue in this fashion until the story has been passed through all the teens. Once this has been completed, compare the final story to the original and take note of all the strange ways in which the story has been changed!

Summarize by pointing out that spreading gossip and rumors leads to inaccurate and ineffective communication because the story gets easily changed and distorted. In other words, paraphrasing, or summarizing another person's story, is a difficult task and it takes hard work to get the story straight. Moreover, the final story usually sounds a lot more drastic than the original. If time permits, ask if any of the teens or if any of their friends were the subject of gossip that was hurtful and inaccurate.

Rumor Mill Story: There was an accident at the intersection of Highways 6 and 49. Three trucks were involved; two of the trucks were semis. One truck was carrying cows, another was carrying chickens, and the third truck was carrying tires. The truck carrying the cows collided with the truck carrying the chickens— 27 chickens were injured; none was killed. The cows were OK, but one of the truck drivers injured his left arm, and 102 tires spilled all over the road.

Cofacilitators are free to make up a story. Note that the story should contain a fair bit of detail and be sufficiently "juicy" to offer youths the temptation of embellishing the facts!

Attending Exercise

Instruction Cards

1. Have the participants break off into dyads (again, have them partner with someone they know the least or have not worked with yet).
2. Hand out the description of *nonattending* behaviors to both partners (let them think they are getting different instructions).
3. Have the participants carry on a 2- to 4-minute conversation, following the *nonattending* instructions.
4. Stop the conversation.
5. Hand out a description of *attending* behaviors to both partners of each dyad (again, let them think they are getting different instructions).
6. Have the participants carry on a 2- to 4-minute conversation following the *attending* behavior instructions.
7. After the *nonattending* and *attending* portions of the exercise have been completed, reconvene the group and discuss.

Note: There should be *no discussion* between the *nonattending* exercise and the *attending* exercise. Ask the students to hang on to their thoughts and feelings about the exercise until the end (debriefing).

Debriefing

During this debriefing, focus on

1. Their feelings, reactions, and so on to both the negative and the positive attending styles (note the definite contrast)
2. How little time it took for their reactions to set in (in most cases, about 60 seconds was enough time)
3. The intensity of their reactions

While doing this, emphasize how expert they are at reading nonverbal behaviors. Maybe they are not aware that they are doing it, but at some level they are really watching and interpreting.

Be supportive and sensitive as they share their feelings. They will usually pull examples from their own lives; allow and encourage them to do this. While they are doing that, focus and support their feelings.

4. What specific behaviors did they see and what assumptions did they make?

Help them get really specific, that is, eyes, hands, head, sighs, and so on. While doing this, get them to model the specific behavior(s) they are describing (facilitator may also model some behavior(s)—use humor).

When they run out, the facilitator models any behaviors not mentioned.

A focus of this exercise, as well as the other exercises, is to develop awareness and to allow the youths to discuss and integrate the information in a nonthreatening manner.

Say something like this: If we were writing a communication book, we could now write a whole chapter on nonverbal communication (praise and encouragement).

Examples of Behavior Descriptions

a. Adopt a *nonattending* position (violate the rules of attending):
   • Turn away; avoid eye contact.
   • Fiddle with your watch, yawn, adjust your clothes, and so on.
   • Look bored.
   • Be so relaxed you look almost asleep, or sit very rigid.

b. Adopt an *attending* position (look interested and pay attention to what the other person has to say):

• *Face* the person.	Face person
• Maintain good *eye* contact.	Eye contact
• *Lean* toward the other person.	Lean in
• Have an *open* posture.	Open posture
• Have a *relaxed/receptive* posture.	Relaxed posture

(SOURCE: From R. Carr & G. Saunders, 1981, *Peer Counseling Starter Kit.* Victoria, BC: Peer Systems Consulting Group, Inc. Adapted with permission of the publisher.)

Fold here

Instruction Card

a. Violate the rules of attending:

- Turn away; avoid eye contact.

- Fiddle with your watch, yawn, adjust your clothes, and so on.

- Look bored.

- Be so relaxed you look almost asleep, or sit very rigid.

Fold here

Instruction Card

b. Look interested and pay attention to what the other person has
   to say:

   • *Face* the person.

   • Maintain good *eye* contact.

   • *Lean* toward the other person.

   • Have an *open* posture.

   • Have a *relaxed/receptive* posture.

SESSION
5

Defining Powerful Relationships:
Assertiveness Instead of Aggressiveness

GOALS

To begin to understand the context in which woman abuse occurs and its effect on women and children
To develop further assertiveness skills

SUMMARY OF OBJECTIVES

I. Check-in
II. Recap
III. *Break the Cycle* Video
IV. Historical Context
V. Questions
VI. Assertiveness

RESOURCES

Break the Cycle video
Discussion questions
Historical context handout
DESC material
Guidelines for guest speakers

NOTES: _____

_____

_____

_____

_____

_____

_____

_____

Defining Powerful Relationships
Activity Plan

*Cofacilitators'
Notes*

This session continues the discussion of woman abuse through the use of the video *Break the Cycle*. Because this video may elicit personal and emotional reactions from the teens, we have included a fairly detailed note to cofacilitators regarding preparation for viewing the video. *It is important that facilitators read this section carefully.* Sufficient and sensitive handling of this material is an important way of letting the teens know that this group is a safe atmosphere in which to discuss violence.

The second focus of this session is on further development of assertiveness skills. The DESC assertiveness training procedure is taught in the second half of the session. In subsequent sessions, it would be appropriate to address conflicts as they arise in the group using DESC to resolve the conflict. This will help the youths learn to confront others and to be confronted in a safe and appropriate manner. Practicing this skill in naturally occurring situations (i.e., conflicts) during the group will also increase the likelihood that the youths will be skilled and confident in resolving conflicts outside of the group. Facilitators can role model the use of DESC by applying it when, for example, the facilitators are feeling frustrated by inattention.

TIME FRAME
(115 program minutes)

ACTIVITIES

(10 min)   I   Check in. Ask members to include examples of opportunities they have had during the past week to practice their active

listening skills (empathy, clarification, paraphrasing) or to notice internal and/or external cues of emotions.

(10 min)   II   Recap.

(45 min)   III   *Break the Cycle* Video: Introduce the video as a film that provides personal comments and testimonials from an abuser, victims, and family members who witnessed abuse. Approximately 15 minutes of discussion should follow the video. Preparation guidelines and suggested discussion questions are provided (see the Session 5 exercises).

(5 min)   IV   Historical Context of Violence Against Women: Information on this topic is provided (see the Session 5 exercises). This topic flows naturally from the last suggested discussion question for the *Break the Cycle* video.

(10 min)   Break

(15 min)   V   Preparation for the Guest Speakers: Ask the youths to prepare questions for next session's speakers (a survivor of woman abuse and a former batterer, or advocates from a women's shelter and a men's counseling center). This can be done individually, in pairs, or in small groups. Some questions may arise naturally from the viewing and/or discussion of *Break the Cycle*. Once the teens have prepared at least one question each, ask them to report back to the large group to screen out duplicate and inappropriate (i.e., insensitive) questions.

Finish by discussing with the youths the courage that it takes for the speakers to come to the group to share with them their experiences of abuse. Emphasize the importance of treating the speakers with respect and dignity by listening attentively, respecting differences of opinion, and asking questions in a respectful manner. It may be appropriate to choose one of the youths to thank the speakers after their presentations. This could be rehearsed with the youth for 5 minutes following the session, or briefly before the start of the next session.

VI   Assertiveness:

(5 min)   a.   Begin this section by making the following two points about being assertive:

- Being assertive does not ensure that we will always get what we want, but it can be satisfying to have expressed ourselves.

- Depending on the situation, it is a personal decision about whether or not it is worth the energy of being assertive (e.g., if someone gives you a dirty look on the bus, it may be best to ignore him or her).

(20 min)   b. Role-play situations using the DESC material (see the Session 5 exercises). Encourage the teens to use situations from their personal inventories or have them role-play a more recent conflict. In the beginning, it usually works best if each youth role-plays him- or herself and the facilitator plays the part of the adversary from the youth's conflict. Also, in the beginning, it works best to do this as a full group exercise because the teens can learn from one another and help each other out if they get stuck and do not know what to do or say.

EXERCISES

Preparation for Viewing *Break the Cycle* Video

The *Break the Cycle* video provides information and some moving testimonials from a battered woman, a batterer, and three teens who grew up with violence in their home.

It is expected that facilitators will view the video in advance. This will ensure that you have had the opportunity to react to the video and to prepare for the reactions of the youths.

Be sensitive to the needs of some teens in the group who may have grown up with violence in their own homes and for whom this video conjures up very uncomfortable feelings. Reactions arising from these feelings may include tears, feigned boredom, inappropriate laughing or jokes, inattentiveness, emotional withdrawal from the group, and anger. It is important to remember that these reactions are a legitimate way for teens to cope with material that may be emotionally loaded.

Prior to viewing the video, give the youths permission to leave the room at any time during the video if they are uncomfortable. Point out to the youths that many of us grew up with violence and discuss the importance of being sensitive to the needs of those around them when watching the video.

If there is a problem with inappropriate laughter or inattentiveness and you feel that it stems from the teens' discomfort with the material, take the time to discuss these reactions:

- Where they come from

- Why we sometimes laugh or make jokes when we are uncomfortable or feeling bad

- What the effect of laughter is on ourselves, others in the room

- What a more appropriate response may be either immediately (if the behavior is very disruptive) or subsequent to the viewing of the video

Because the video focuses on wife assault, cofacilitators should also be prepared for reactions of male defensiveness. Note that this reaction may come from both the young men *and* the young women in the group. *It is best to address male defensiveness openly,* and therefore it is included as one of the discussion questions for the video. Gender-specific statistics and discussions of socially based power imbalances and the historical context of violence against women are helpful ways of showing how the flow of violence moves largely from men toward women and children. Please refer to the introduction of this manual for ways of dealing with male defensiveness in the group.

Break the Cycle: *Suggested Discussion Questions*

1. Any reactions to the video?

   If necessary, probe: Did you like the video—why or why not? How did you feel while watching the video?

2. Were the people in the video believable? If not, why not?

   Note that many people have a difficult time believing the testimony of the battered woman because she appears too assertive to be an abuse victim. This provides a good opportunity to discuss the myth that only women who are unassertive or have low self-esteem are affected by woman abuse.

3. How did living with wife assault affect the teenagers in the film?

   The two teen girls and the teen boy all react somewhat differently; discuss these differences.

4. Why do you think the teen boy in the video abuses his girlfriend when he talks about how horrible it was growing up with violence in his home?

5. What is your reaction to the teen boy's description of the violent incident in which he broke his girlfriend's ribs?

   Emphasize how he takes no responsibility for his actions and tries to blame the girlfriend for the incident. Note that he focuses on himself, his embarrassment, and his inconvenience, and that he seems totally lacking in empathy. You may wish to have the youths think back to the session when empathy was discussed and explore how some empathy would have made a difference in this situation.

6. What factors made it difficult for the women in the video to get out of violent relationships (police response; response of neighbors; staying for the sake of the children; lack of support from the parents of the battered women; lack of financial resources, that is, dependent on partner; socialization, or society's expectations of a wife and mother; and so on)?

7. We did not see many wealthy families in the video. Is that because violence only happens in poor families?

   No: Wealthy families may be less likely to go public and speak about the violence in their families.

8. Why does the video focus on wife assault? Why do you think there were no testimonials from battered men?

The youth may raise these issues on their own. If they do not, most are probably thinking about it—this is predictable male defensiveness that can be experienced by both men and women.

This is a good opportunity to discuss:

- The prevalence rates in official reports of the abuse of women and children in families (e.g., 90% of police occurrences of domestic violence involve the abuse of women and children)

- The power imbalance in North American society that gives men more social power and encourages men to exercise that power over women and children

- The physical size differential between most men and women in North America that results in men's acts of violence inflicting more damage and their threats of violence being more intimidating, which gives them more power, which some men choose to abuse to control women

Also emphasize that it is never OK to use violence. Some women are violent and this is not acceptable either.

DESC

DESC are the initials of a four-step breakdown of an assertive statement: describe, express, specify, consequences (Bower & Bower, 1976).

(D) DESCRIBE exactly the other person's behavior that is bothersome or of interest to me.

(E) EXPRESS how this behavior affects me.

(S) SPECIFY exactly what behavior I want the other person to do.

(C) CONSEQUENCES—what I would be prepared to do in return.

We have found that adolescents have a difficult time remembering and applying the DESC acronym. Consequently, when using the DESC protocol, we tend to shift the focus away from the DESC acronym and concentrate on the second part of the protocol, the DESC script:

(D) When you . . .

(E) I feel . . .

(S) I want you to . . .

(C) Then I would . . . and you would . . .

When teaching youth the DESC method, you may want to omit the DESC acronym and begin with the DESC script (which you may wish to refer to as an "assertiveness script").

Begin this exercise by posting the DESC script on a piece of flip chart paper. Explain that these four statements are the basic tools for assertive communication. Ask for volunteers to try using the DESC script first to state a criticism and, second, to state a compliment.

When the youth seem to have grasped the concept, have them apply the DESC script to their Personal Anger Inventories or a recent conflict, with one of the cofacilitators playing the role of the adversary.

Violence Against Women—A Historical Context

(SOURCES: Frost-Knappman, 1994; Olsen, 1994)

It is important to examine the historical roots of violence and discrimination against women because the residue of many of these practices contributes to the attitudes and beliefs about women today.

3000-2000 B.C.	In most parts of the world, female slaves are subject to the master's sexual whims.
2000-1000 B.C.	A woman can divorce her husband for cruelty. A woman who hates her husband enough to deprive him of sex may be released from her marriage, but only if she is entirely blameless and her husband has talked against her "greatly."
735 B.C.	Women are defined as possessions of husbands, and husbands have the right to beat or kill their wives.
1200 A.D.	Wife beating is common in Europe and is endorsed by the church as the loving husband's means of correcting his wife's faults.
1300-1400	English law allows men to beat their wives for the purpose of "lawful and reasonable correction." Women are all seen as dangerous and sexually insatiable; the vice of lust is usually depicted as female.
1500-1600	In England, women who transgress the bounds of acceptable feminine behavior are punished for their boldness. A woman is tied to a "ducking stool," suspended from a beam, and dunked repeatedly into the nearest body of water.
1767	British Common Law allows for the "rule of thumb"—a man can chastise his wife with a whip or stick no greater than the width of his thumb. Abuse is therefore legislated.
1920	Sweden's new Marriage Code ends guardianship of wives by husbands and makes wives legal adults at age 21.
1970s	Until this time in United States, aggravated assault against a stranger was a felony by law, but assaulting a spouse was a misdemeanor.
1977	Of 9,000 rapes reported in West Germany this year, 850 resulted in convictions. Wives are beaten in an estimated 5 million German families.

1978   One rape occurs every hour in London, England.

1978   John Rideout, the first man indicted in the United States for marital rape, is acquitted, although he admits to having beaten his wife. At least 14% of U.S. wives are raped by their husbands.

1980   The FBI estimates that a rape occurs every 6 minutes in the United States, noting that many rapes are not reported and neglecting to include marital rape in its statistics. At least half of all rape victims are attacked by people they know. Arrests are made in 38% of reported rape cases.

1981   Duluth, Minnesota, becomes the first city to institute mandatory arrests in domestic disputes.

1982   Marital, anal, and oral rape are outlawed in Canada.

1983   Controversy erupts in Brazil after a woman is sentenced to 14 years for killing her husband, while a man who killed his wife is given a 2-year suspended sentence on the grounds that he was "defending his honor."

1991   More adult women in the United States are injured by battery than by any other cause.

1991   Great Britain repeals an 18th-century law sanctioning marital rape.

SESSION
6

Date Rape: Being Clear, Being Safe

GOALS	To hear speakers talk about their experiences of woman abuse
	To begin to explore sexual assault and date rape

SUMMARY OF OBJECTIVES	RESOURCES
I. Check-in	Guest speakers
II. Recap	The Dance Exercise
III. Guest Speakers	
IV. Sexual Assault	
V. Practice Assertiveness Skills	

NOTES: _____

_____

_____

_____

_____

_____

_____

_____

_____

_____

SESSION
6

Date Rape
Activity Plan

Cofacilitators'
Notes

The presentation by the guest speakers during this session is frequently cited by participants as the most interesting and informative part of the whole program. If you have any doubts as to the handling of this portion of the program, it is suggested that you ask a woman's advocate and a counselor from a men's counseling program to speak instead. Please review the protocols for this session found in the "Exercises" section of Session 6.

The topic of sexual assault is also introduced during this session. Youths are provided with a sexual assault scenario and, after some discussion, are given an opportunity to rehearse some of their assertiveness skills in role-playing an appropriate response to the scenario. Participants are also asked to define sexual assault given that one of the responsibilities of men and women is to know what constitutes sexual assault.

TIME FRAME
(120 program minutes)

ACTIVITIES

(10 min)   I   Check in. Ask members to include examples of opportunities they have had during the past week to practice their assertiveness skills (i.e., DESC) or active listening skills (empathy, clarification, paraphrasing) or to notice internal and/or external cues of emotions.

(10 min)   II   Recap.

III Presentations by Guest Speakers:

(20 min)   a. Presentation by a Survivor of Woman Abuse: A brief (5-10 min) presentation by a survivor of woman abuse or, alternatively, an advocate from the local women's shelter or advocacy center is followed by an open discussion. The youths can pose the questions they prepared last session along with any other questions that arise during the discussion. It may be appropriate for one of the youths to thank the speaker and present her with an honorarium (enclosed in a thank you note, signed by the youth).

(20 min)   b. Presentation by a Former Batterer: A brief (5-10 min) presentation by a former batterer or, alternatively, a counselor from a local batterers' program. The teens can pose the questions they prepared last session along with any other questions that arise during the discussion. Again, it may be appropriate for one of the youths to thank the speaker and present him with an honorarium (enclosed in a thank you note, signed by the youth).

(10 min)   c. Debriefing: Once the speakers have left, provide a brief opportunity for the youths to discuss their reactions to the presentations by the speakers, and to ask any questions that they were not comfortable asking the speakers themselves.

(10 min)   Break

(20 min)   IV Sexual Assault

Preamble: We are going to be talking about sexual assault: what it is and what we can do about it.

Read the handout "The Dance" (see Session 6 exercises) and lead a discussion with the teenagers based on the discussion guide provided. Alternatively, most of the discussion questions could be assigned to the teens to work on in pairs and then report back to the larger group for further discussion.

(20 min)   V Practicing Assertiveness Skills

Active Listening: Remind the youths that we practiced using active listening skills in a previous session. Ask if they remember why active listening is important. The following should be included among their responses:

- It allows us to be clear on what others mean.
- It shows the other person that we are listening and that we care about his or her perspective/opinion (empathy).
- It helps to encourage assertive responses.

In pairs, ask the youths to role-play the scenario from "The Dance" using active listening and assertiveness skills. Explore how the outcome changed and ask the youths to identify specific reasons as to why the outcome changed.

EXERCISES	## Cofacilitator Background and Preparation Material for Hiring Guest Speakers

Cofacilitators should note that this process requires a fair amount of thought and preparation. In particular, we encourage you to consult with and develop strong liaisons with relevant community agencies (e.g., men's counseling programs for batterers, battered women's shelters or advocacy centers). Moreover, we suggest that you follow this protocol only if you feel that the appropriate safeguards are in place and if you have the support of local community agencies.

Background: Benefits of Survivors and Former Batterers as Speakers

Across the past 5 years, teens have consistently reported that these presentations were a highlight of the program. For some youths, it seems that these presentations are salient because the youths identify with the speaker, either as a victim or perpetrator in an abusive intimate relationship, or as the son or daughter of an abusive father (or stepfather or boyfriend). For these young people, the speakers provide a powerful and hopeful model for change in what is frequently described as a hopeless situation. For other teens who have limited firsthand experience with men's violence, it helps them understand the reality of men's violence and how the abuse of men's social power plays itself out in intimate relationships. The presentations are also highly instrumental in breaking down the myths of woman abuse. For example, both youths with and without experiences in abusive relationships have come to understand why women stay in an abusive relationship, and recognize that the situation does not originate from the victim's response but from the batterer's behavior. A final benefit of employing survivors of woman abuse and former batterers as presenters is that it provides an outlet for survivors and former batterers who are interested in participating in social action toward ending violence against women.

Concerns Regarding Employing Survivors and Former Batterers as Speakers

In spite of a number of benefits, this process is not without controversy. Listed below are a number of potential concerns regarding the employment of survivors and former batterers as speakers that may be important for you to consider:

1. Can we have presentations in a way that does not exploit women with histories of abuse (as do some talk show hosts) and in a way that facilitates real social change?

2. Are the survivors and former batterers at a point in their personal process where this form of social action is advantageous to both themselves and the youths?

3. Are the youths at a point in their learning process such that an atmosphere of respect, comfort, and support is present for both the speaker and the youths during the presentation?

4. Are the youths and the speakers sufficiently informed such that the primary focus of the discussion is the examination of the consequences of the abuse of men's power in relationships as well as the stimulation of change in the youths' relationships?

5. Do the presenters have sufficient support systems in place?

6. Will a counselor from the batterers' program attend the presentation? (A good working relationship with a men's counseling program is especially important because you will be relying on them to suggest appropriate speakers and because they too will be asked to attend the talk.)

7. Has a counselor from the batterers' program checked with the former batterer's current partner to ensure that he is still nonabusive in his relationship?

8. Do the presenters have previous experience speaking to groups on this topic? If yes, have reference checks regarding previous speaking engagements been made? If no, what training does the presenter have to prepare him or her for this type of talk? Is the training adequate?

Once again, if any of these concerns has not been adequately addressed, we suggest that you ask a representative from a women's shelter and one from a batterers' counseling program to speak to the teens instead. If, however, you decide to hire speakers, we have included a step-by-step guideline for arranging the talks.

Preparation for Speakers

1. Ensure that as a facilitator you are clear on and comfortable with the myths and facts of wife assault, the definitions of *violence* and *power*, and the goals and the objectives of the presentation. If you have any concerns or questions, refer to the material in your manual, the handouts from the training session, and relevant parts of the training video or call the YRP office or a women's advocate in your community.

2. Contact the local women's shelter and batterers' program to inquire whether or not they are aware of any survivors and

former batterers who do presentations on this topic. Ask how to contact these individuals and for any references they can provide regarding the training and previous public speaking experience of these individuals.

3. If you will be using a former batterer, ensure that he has "successfully" completed a batterers' program. It has been suggested in our own community that this person should have stopped his violent behavior for at least 1 year, as a way of ensuring that the term *former* batterer really is appropriate. Also, ask your contact person at this program to do a partner check to ensure that the former batterer is still nonviolent. Ask if a counselor from the program will be able to attend the presentation.

4. Send the information sheet and contract provided in the manual to the potential speakers. You may wish to add your own personal cover letter to this package. You should also note that speakers are paid for their time. We suggest an honorarium of $50.00 for each speaker.

5. Arrange for a meeting with the potential speaker to discuss the objectives and goals of the program and the presentation, possible topics to include for discussion, topics not appropriate for discussion (e.g., child sexual abuse experiences), the contract, concerns that the presenter may have, and possible questions and reactions of the teens. You should also give the presenters an opportunity to practice responding to backlash comments or questions. It is also important to ask the survivor of woman abuse if she has any safety needs that should be arranged before the presentation (e.g., if there is someone she would like to bring with her, whether she would be more comfortable speaking on a different day than the batterer).

6. If you or the speaker have any concerns regarding the presentation, do not proceed with the presentation. Either find a more suitable speaker or consider the use of an alternative medium such as a counselor from the batterers' program or a women's advocate.

7. If the meeting is satisfactory to yourself and the potential presenter, get the required signatures on the contract.

8. Ensure that the material from Sessions 1 to 5 has been adequately covered in the group prior to the presentation.

By this time in the program, you should also have completed the following list of especially salient exercises:

• Discussion of myths and facts of woman abuse
• Viewing and discussion of the video *Break the Cycle*
• Defining *violence* and *power*
• Discussion of power and control in relationships

9. Prepare the teens for the presentation: (a) Have the youths prepare questions for the speaker; (b) discuss with the youths the importance of having a respectful discussion with the speaker on the issues involved; (c) ask one of the youths to thank the speaker and rehearse this with him or her (the youths may also present the speaker with the payment).

10. Arrange to meet with the speakers within 1 or 2 weeks after the presentation to provide them with feedback regarding the presentation. Alternatively, feedback could be provided in correspondence.

Information for Presenters (Female Speaker)

The Youth Relationship Program is a group approach with adolescents whose purpose is the prevention of woman abuse and interpersonal violence. The goal of the program is to help youth to understand the abuse of power and control in their own relationships, and to promote the development of more egalitarian relationships. One way in which the program attempts to meet this goal is through the presentation of guest speakers who are survivors of woman abuse and former batterers (who have successfully completed a batterers' program).

The survivors are asked to provide information on one or more of the following topics: why women stay in abusive relationships (e.g., isolation, social stigma, fear); personal resources, or lack thereof; community resources, or lack thereof; what the early warning signs of an abusive partner are; escalation of the violence in their relationship; how they were affected by the violence; the personal consequences of various types of abuse (e.g., emotional and psychological versus physical); how their children were affected by the violence; backlash (e.g., victim blaming; "What about women's violence?"); safety plans; how they got out of the relationship; and potential social action by youth. We ask that the presenters adhere to topics related to violence by an intimate partner. This is not an appropriate forum for discussing other types of abuse such as child (sexual or physical) abuse.

The presentation should provide a positive experience for both the youths and the presenter. The presentation should be a comfortable fit with the presenter's goals for working toward social change. Furthermore, we recognize that this is a difficult topic and ask presenters whether they have an adequate support system in place.

Contract for Presenters (Female Speaker)

As part of social action toward the prevention of violence against women, and in exchange for an honorarium of _____, I agree to give a 20-minute presentation to the YRP group that is consistent with the following guidelines:

1. The purpose for the presentation is to stimulate social action and, in particular, to help youths create change toward the prevention of woman abuse on an individual and community level.
2. The central topic is abuse of women in intimate relationships. (The discussion of child abuse is not an appropriate topic for this forum.)
3. The message is consistent with the YRP view that violence in intimate relationships is a result of men's abuse of their social power and privilege and that men are fully responsible for their behavior.

I understand that the YRP cofacilitators will be responsible for the following:

1. Educating the youths on the topics that will be discussed
2. Asking the youths to prepare questions to ask the speaker
3. Providing a safe and respectful atmosphere for both the youths and the speaker
4. Providing the presenter with feedback subsequent to the presentation

_____   _____   _____
Name of Presenter (Print)   Signature   Date

_____   _____   _____
Name of Cofacilitator (Print)   Signature   Date

Information for Presenters (Male Speaker)

The YRP program is a group approach with adolescents whose purpose is the prevention of woman abuse and interpersonal violence. The goal of the program is to help youth to understand the abuse of power and control in their own relationships, and to promote the development of more egalitarian relationships. One way in which the program attempts to meet this goal is through the presentation of guest speakers who are survivors of woman abuse and former batterers (who have successfully completed a batterers' program).

The former batterers provide information on one or more of the following topics: why they were violent (emphasizing personal choice); myths of woman abuse (not caused by alcohol, drugs, anger control problem, stress, and so on); types of abuse they found themselves using; the process of change (how they stopped being violent); how the violence affected their children; backlash (e.g., victim blaming; "What about women's violence?"); and stimulation of discussion of what young people can do. We ask that the presenters adhere to topics related to violence by an intimate partner. This is not an appropriate forum to discuss other types of abuse such as child (sexual or physical) abuse.

The presentation should be a positive experience for both the youths and the presenter. The presentation should be a comfortable fit with the presenter's goals for working toward social change. Furthermore, we recognize that this is a difficult topic and ask presenters whether they have an adequate support system in place. We ask that a counselor from the batterers' program attend the presentation with the former batterer. We also require someone from the batterers' program to check with the former batterer's current partner to ensure the former batterer is still nonviolent.

Contract for Presenters (Male Speaker)

As part of social action toward the prevention of violence against women, and in exchange for an honorarium of _____, I agree to give a 20-minute presentation to the YRP group that is consistent with the following guidelines:

1. The purpose for the presentation is to stimulate social action and, in particular, to help youths create change toward the prevention of woman abuse on an individual and community level.
2. The central topic is the abuse of women in intimate relationships. (The discussion of child abuse is not an appropriate topic for this forum.)
3. The message is consistent with the YRP view that violence in intimate relationships is a result of men's abuse of their social power and privilege and that men are fully responsible for their behavior.

I understand that the YRP will be responsible for the following:

1. Educating the youths on the topics that will be discussed
2. Asking the youths to prepare questions to ask the speaker
3. Provision of a safe and respectful atmosphere for both the youths and the speaker
4. Provision of the presenter with feedback subsequent to the presentation

_____   _____   _____
Name of Presenter (Print)   Signature   Date

_____   _____   _____
Name of Cofacilitator (Print)   Signature   Date

_____   _____   _____
Name of Counselor (Print)   Signature   Date

The Dance

Jamie and Lori are at a school dance. They have been going out for almost 2 months. After a while, Jamie asks Lori to come outside with him because it's too hot in the gym. Lori is glad to get out for a bit.

Outside, they are talking and laughing. They notice no one is around and so they start kissing. In a few minutes, Jamie suggests they go out behind the bleachers in case somebody interrupts them. Lori says she'd rather go inside now—their friends will wonder where they've gone.

"C'mon," Jamie says, "they probably haven't even noticed we left."

"Only for a minute then," Lori says.

Behind the bleachers, they pick up where they left off. After a few minutes of kissing, Jamie touches Lori's breast over her clothes. Lori pulls his hand off, gives Jamie a kiss, and says, "Maybe we should go inside now."

Jamie says, "It's too much fun out here" and presses Lori against the bleachers. Lori starts to move away but Jamie holds her and, kissing her, he again touches her breast.

Lori pushes Jamie away, and crying, she says, "Why can't you just stop?!!"

Lori runs into the school.

The Dance: Discussion Guide

1. What are your reactions to the story? Prompt the following:
   - Does Jamie like Lori?
   - Does Lori like Jamie?
   - What do you think Jamie wanted?
   - What do you think Lori wanted?
   - How do you think she was feeling up to the point when she ran?
   - How do you think he was feeling up to this point?

2. Was this a sexual assault? Define sexual assault. (Emphasize during the discussion that one of the responsibilities of men and women is to know what constitutes sexual assault.)

3. Did Lori indicate she was not interested in sex? If yes, when?

4. Does the story provide any negative messages about men and women? If yes, are these messages accurate (or "real")?

5. Generalizing:

   Sometimes people say that "a woman was asking for it" because of what she was wearing. What do you think about that? Have the teens identify other victim-blaming statements and discuss them.

Often, guys don't understand how this kind of pressure affects girls. What do you think?

How does this story fit with the socialization we receive while growing up about how to "Act Like a Lady" and "Act Like a Man?"

6. Personal rights and responsibilities:

In earlier sessions, we discussed personal rights and personal responsibilities.

- What personal rights are being violated in this situation?
- What responsibilities does Jamie have in this situation?
- What responsibilities does Lori have?
- Did each of them carry out these responsibilities?

The Contexts of Relationship Violence

These five sessions expand the intimate violence issue to the larger societal and cultural contexts, including gender socialization, peer pressure, and media influences. When we look at the toys most children want and play with, people in school who are popular, television and films, and current music, we can clearly see how society reinforces violence. Mottos like "take what you can get," "look out for number 1," "she had it coming to her," and "sex sells" show us the extent to which violence has become a part of our mind-sets—so much so that we hardly even notice the violence, until we stop to take a look. This section enables youths to stop and take that critical look at the many sources encouraging violence in our society. One of the things that youths gain in this section is the understanding that everyone is at risk for relationship violence by virtue of living in this "culture of violence."

Partly at issue in gender-based violence is gender-based negative attitudes such as sexism, sex role stereotypes, and gender role rigidity. Teens are encouraged to examine how our notions of "maleness" and "femaleness" are formed, and to consider critically their own specific definitions and how they relate to developing healthy interpersonal relationships. In one example, these conceptions and misconceptions are discussed as part of the teens' decision making in choosing a partner.

Once again, teens are given the opportunity to counter these negative attitudes and the incorrect information about intimate violence and men's and women's roles in intimate relationships, adding further practice to their antiviolence relationships' skill building. The final session in this section (Session 11) contains a popular and dramatic activity. In the "Sleazy Talk Show" exercise, youths are provided with the opportunity to verbalize the expertise they have gained about interpersonal violence. The misinformed, yet relentless opinions of the counterexpert, Dr. Brutal (played by the facilitator), are a fun yet challenging way of getting at the attitudinal and informational issues. The powerful video *Dreamworlds* enables youths to view the sophistication with which the media achieves their gender-based portrayals of men and women. By the close of this section, youths will be better equipped to recognize the various societal and cultural obstacles to changing violence in relationships.

SESSION
7

Date Rape and Learning How to Handle Dating Pressure

GOALS	To further explore sexual assault; our rights and responsibilities in dating relationships
	To practice assertiveness skills for handling dating pressure

---

SUMMARY OF OBJECTIVES	RESOURCES
I. Check-in II. Recap III. *Date Rape* Video IV. Practice Assertiveness Skills	*Date Rape* video Ending Sexual Assault handout

---

NOTES: _____

_____

_____

_____

_____

_____

_____

_____

Date Rape and Learning How to Handle Dating Pressure
Activity Plan

*Cofacilitators'
Notes*

Following the recap, facilitators should inform the group that the topic for today is a continuation of the discussion of sexual assault and that there will be a video on the topic. Participants are reminded to take care of themselves and to take a break during the session if needed as well as to be respectful of those around them. A facilitator should briefly check on any individual who may leave to see if he or she needs assistance. Given that a number of participants may be victims of sexual assault/abuse, these procedures are particularly important.

This is a very full session. Consequently, facilitators will want to be careful to keep the check-in and recap very brief and watch the clock for each exercise.

TIME FRAME
(120 program minutes)

ACTIVITIES

(10 min)	I	Check in.
(10 min)	II	Recap.
(50 min)	III	*Date Rape* Video.
(10 min)		Break

(15 min)   Discussion of the *Date Rape* video should include the following:

- How did you feel in response to the video?

- How would you define date rape?

- What did Gary want? What did Samantha want?

- Did he get any early signals that she did, or did not, want to have sex? Did he listen? Did he ask her what she wanted?

- Name all the active listening skills you can remember and consider whether or not he used these skills.

- How might the use of active listening skills have made a difference?

- What responsibilities discussed in previous sessions were not carried out? What responsibilities did Gary have? his friends? his father? Sam? her friends? her parents?

- Discuss taking responsibility for our behavior and make connections to the "just deserts" belief (e.g., women are asking to be assaulted if they act or dress in certain ways).

(15 min)   IV Practicing Assertiveness Skills

Taking Responsibility for My Behavior When I Have Made a Mistake: Discuss with the group the importance of assertively taking responsibility for our own behavior by using examples from the *Date Rape* video. Have the youths role-play what it would look like if Gary had taken responsibility for his abusive behavior. What conversation might he have had with Samantha?

(15 min)   *Responding to Victim-Blaming Statements and Sexual Assault Myths* (see Session 5): Provide youths with victim-blaming statements and myths of sexual assault. Ask the youths to brainstorm prosocial responses to these comments. This exercise works well by dividing youths into two groups and having them come together as a full group later to share their answers.

EXERCISES

Ending Sexual Assault: Responsibilities of
Men and Women in Dating Relationships

For Women:

1. Set clear sexual limits before the date begins and communicate those limits. Be clear, honest, and consistent in your verbal and nonverbal communications about sexual desires and limits.
2. Get out of a dangerous situation as soon as you sense the danger. Trust your instincts.
3. Be assertive. Don't let yourself be put in vulnerable situations.
4. Keep in mind that alcohol and drugs impair your judgment.
5. Know which behaviors constitute sexual assault.

For Men:

1. Don't put pressure on a woman to have sex. You can have a successful social encounter without "scoring."
2. Don't assume you know what a woman wants and vice versa.
3. Speak up if you feel you're getting a double message from a woman. If you are still confused, don't have sex with her.
4. Keep in mind that alcohol and drugs impair your judgment.
5. Know which behaviors constitute sexual assault.

(SOURCE: From *Date Sexual Assault* (pamphlet). Reprinted with permission of the Sexual Assault Center, London, Ontario.)

Defining Sexual Assault

Assault: The intentional use of force on another person against his or her will. Touching, slapping, kicking, punching, or pushing are all examples of assault.

It is also an assault to *threaten* to use force. For instance, if someone threatens to beat you up, this can be an assault even if the threat is not carried out.

Sexual Assault: Any unwanted sexual act imposed on one person by another.

A person may be charged if you were forced to kiss, fondle, or have sexual intercourse with the person or you were kissed or touched in a sexual way without your consent (with no sign of physical injury or abuse).

Sexual Assault With a Weapon: Sexual assault with the use of a weapon (either an imitation or a real weapon) or with the threat to use a weapon.

Sexual Assault Causing Bodily Harm: The victim was physically hurt during the sexual assault.

A person could also be charged if he or she threatened to hurt a third party (such as the victim's child) or if he or she was with someone who sexually assaulted another.

Aggravated Sexual Assault: The victim was wounded, crippled, disfigured, or brutally beaten during the sexual assault. The victim's life was endangered.

Date Rape: Date rape is sexual assault that occurs in a dating or social situation.

Victim-Blaming Statements

Her dress was tight.
She was asking for it.
She had sex with me before.
Women say no when they really mean yes.
She was drunk; she didn't care.
I paid for everything; what did she expect?
She's done it before with other guys.

Myth and Facts of Sexual Assault

(SOURCE: Ontario Women's Directorate, 1995)

Myth: Sexual assault is most often committed by strangers.

Fact: Women face the greatest risk of sexual assault from men they know, not strangers. Of the women who are sexually assaulted, most are sexually assaulted by men known to them—dates, boyfriends, marital partners, friends, family members, or neighbors.

Myth: The best way for a woman to protect herself from sexual assault is to avoid being alone at night in dark, deserted places, such as alleys or parking lots.

Fact: Most sexual assaults occur in a private home and the large percentage of these occur in the victim's home.

Myth: Women who are sexually assaulted "ask for it" by the way they dress or act.

Fact: Victims of sexual assault report a wide range of dress and actions at the time of the assault. Any woman of any age and physical type, in almost any situation, can be sexually assaulted. No woman ever asks or deserves to be sexually assaulted. Whatever a woman wears, wherever she goes, whomever she talks to, "no" means "no."

Myth: Men of certain races and backgrounds are more likely to sexually assault women.

Fact: Men who commit sexual assault come from every economic, ethnic, racial, age, and social group. The belief that women are more often sexually assaulted by men of color or working-class men is a stereotype rooted in racism and classism.

Myth: It's only sexual assault if physical violence or weapons are used.

Fact: Sexual assault is any unwanted act of a sexual nature imposed by one person on another. Most sexual assaults are committed by a man known to the victim who is likely to use verbal pressure, tricks, and/or threats during an assault.

Myth: Unless she is physically harmed, a sexual assault victim will not suffer any long-term effects.

Fact: Sexual assault can have serious effects on women's health and well-being. Women who have been sexually assaulted feel anger and fear, and can become more cautious and less trusting.

Myth: Women cannot be sexually assaulted by their husbands or boyfriends.

Fact: Women have the right to say no to any form of sex, even in a marriage or dating relationship.

SESSION
8

Gender Socialization and Societal Pressure

| GOALS | To review and strengthen skills learned to date through rehearsal |
| | To solidify group cohesion through acceptance and giving of compliments |

SUMMARY OF OBJECTIVES

I. Check-in
II. Recap
III. Preparing for Conflict
IV. *Power to Choose* Video
V. Warm Fuzzies

RESOURCES

Preparing for Conflict handout
Power to Choose video
Warm Fuzzies Exercise

NOTES: _____

_____

_____

_____

_____

_____

_____

_____

SESSION
8

*Gender Socialization
and Societal Pressure*
Activity Plan

*Cofacilitators'
Notes*

The Power to Choose video is sold with a teacher's guide that
includes discussion questions and activities that may be used in
addition to the exercise listed below.

During this session, there is a Warm Fuzzies exercise that provides an opportunity for participants to express to one another
qualities or characteristics that they admire in the other group
members. This exercise has many purposes. We all appreciate receiving compliments, yet many of us are uncomfortable both accepting
and giving compliments. This exercise provides an opportunity in a
safe environment to practice giving and receiving compliments. It
also fosters group cohesion, which should be fairly well developed
by this point. If not attended to, however, the group cohesion can
erode at any point during the program. This is very destructive to
the group process and to learning in this forum.

TIME FRAME
(110 program minutes)

ACTIVITIES

(10 min)   I   Check in. Ask youths to report if they have had an opportunity
during the past week to use any of the assertiveness skills that
we have been practicing in group, that is, using DESC, active
listening (paraphrasing, empathy, seeking clarification), and
recognizing internal and external affective cues (cues that we
or others are angry, happy, sad, and so on).

116

(10 min)   II Recap.

(15 min)   III Preparing for Conflict handout: Use this handout (see the Session 8 exercises) as a summary of information and skills learned thus far regarding conflict resolution strategies.

Emphasize that our approach to conflict will affect the outcome. If, for example, we believe that conflict helps point out that there is a problem and gives us an opportunity to address this and improve our relationships, we may be less defensive and more constructive in our relationships.

(25 min)   IV *Power to Choose* Video: This video has four scenes depicting different power relationships. To process the video, facilitators may stop between each scene for discussion or view all four scenes with discussion to follow.

(10 min)   Break

(25 min)   Discussion of the video should include prosocial problem solving using feelings rather than blaming the other. List of different examples or methods of conflict resolution, with emphasis on negotiation and win-win or no-lose rather than on power struggles resulting in a win-lose situation. Role-play alternative responses to each of the four scenes. Try to incorporate DESC, active listening skills (empathy, paraphrasing, seeking clarification), and working toward a win-win solution. It works well to divide the group into two or three smaller groups and assign each group one or two of the scenes to role-play. Give each group approximately 10 minutes to prepare their role-play and then have them perform the role-plays for the entire group.

(20 min)   V Warm Fuzzies Exercise: We all like to be paid compliments yet sometimes expressing our positive feelings toward someone and accepting compliments is very difficult for us. Youths especially are often more comfortable teasing and tossing out jibes than they are extending compliments to others. This exercise (see the Session 8 exercises) gives us practice at expressing positive feelings toward others in a very safe (anonymous) manner.

EXERCISES   Preparing for Conflict: Conflict Tips

A.   1. Recognize that we often hear another's comment from a defensive, self-protective stance.

        2. Prepare yourself to listen. Ask yourself how you are feeling (e.g., feeling defensive, insecure, hurt, put down). We learn to cope with these feelings by telling ourselves, "I need to be aware of how my partner is feeling. Some criticisms are justified; I'm not perfect. I have a right to slow down and think."

        3. Identify clearly with your partner the issue to be discussed and maintain focus.

B.   Recognize that many conflicts occur spontaneously and that often partners are caught off balance. It is therefore useful to plan to discuss difficult issues when both partners are calm and sure of the issue to be discussed.

        Asking permission to discuss issues is also useful rather than imposing our own agenda.

C.   It is useful to review how we handled conflict. After arguments, it is useful to ask ourselves some questions:

        a. What new information have I learned?

        b. Did I listen to my partner or did I spend time trying to defend myself?

        c. How do I feel about what has happened?

        d. What is the new position we have arrived at?

        e. What things am I telling myself about the argument? Is this true and does it reflect truly what happened?

Warm Fuzzies Exercise

Provide each youth with a small pad of paper (app. 8 cm × 6 cm or 4" × 3") stapled to a string necklace (several sheets of scrap paper stapled together will suffice). You will need at least one page of paper in the pad for every group member (facilitators included) plus one, because the top page does not get used.

Ask the youths to put the notepad necklace around their necks so that the pad hangs down the back. The participants are then instructed to approach every group member (facilitators included) and write on a page in the pad some quality or characteristic that they admire or like in that person. It is prudent to emphasize that they must only express admiration of *qualities* or *character traits*—not physical attributes. Also emphasize that you are aware that the participants may know some group members better than others, but that you expect that during the past eight sessions they have come to know each other well enough to be able to think of at least one positive quality for each person in the group. Typically, these notations are anonymous; however, if they wish to sign their name, that would be acceptable. The exercise should continue until the participants have written in every group member's notepad. Once this point has been reached, they may remove their notepads and read the notations inside.

It frequently happens that there are one or two group members who (for whatever reason) are not well integrated into the group. It is the facilitators' responsibility to ensure that this/these individual(s) are not left out. The best strategy is usually to approach group members individually and quietly ask, "Have you written in John's notepad yet?"

SESSION
9

Choosing Partners and Sex Role Stereotypes

GOALS	To examine gender role rigidity, the connection between sex role stereotypes and violence, and to explore alternatives

SUMMARY OF OBJECTIVES	RESOURCES
I. Check-in II. Recap III. How We Choose Partners IV. *Right From the Start* Video	*Right From the Start* video

NOTES: _____

_____

_____

_____

_____

_____

_____

_____

_____

SESSION
9

Choosing Partners and Sex Role Stereotypes
Activity Plan

Cofacilitators' Notes

This session explores how we choose dating and marital partners. Often our choices are based on stereotypes of what the ideal man or woman should be. This session examines gender stereotypes, how they influence our behavior, and how they can lead to unhealthy and abusive relationships. The *Right From the Start* video for this session explores these issues and examines behaviors that help to create healthy, nonviolent relationships.

This is the first opportunity provided to split the group into same-gender groups. This is an important dynamic in terms of creating feelings of solidarity among the young men and women in the group and examining gender differences. Splitting the group along gender lines can also foster male defensiveness, however. Be watchful for this, and if this issue arises, be sure to address it directly.

TIME FRAME
(115 program minutes)

ACTIVITIES

(10 min)

I   Check in. Ask the youths to report if they have had an opportunity during the past week to use any of the assertiveness skills that we have been practicing in group, that is, using DESC, active listening (paraphrasing, empathy, seeking clarification), and recognizing internal and external affective cues (cues that we or others are angry, happy, sad, and so on).

(10 min)   II Recap.

(25 min)   III How We Choose Partners: Divide into gender groups and have teens come up with three lists:

    1. Qualities they look for in a best friend

    2. Qualities they look for in a dating partner

    3. Qualities they look for in a husband/wife

As a full group, compare and contrast lists:

- How do each of the three lists differ for males versus females?

- How do the guys feel about the qualities that the girls claim to be looking for in a boyfriend and husband?

- How do the girls feel about the guys' lists?

- What are the similarities and differences between the lists for best friend versus girlfriend and husband/wife? Should these lists be dissimilar?

Also discuss the following:

- What do you notice about these lists?

- Are these roles realistic? Can each of us be all of these things?

- How can these roles get us in trouble (e.g., boys not able to express emotions except anger, girls not able to express anger and be assertive, limits on who we can be, and so on)?

- Who has more power?

(10 min)   Break

(25 min)   IV *Right From the Start* Video: In introducing the video, participants are told that we will be watching a video about abuse in teen relationships. Mention that the video will pull together a lot of the strategies that we have discussed during the group about preventing date rape. Ask the participants to make note of these strategies during the video. Also ask them to watch for gender stereotypes that can lead to abusive relationships.

(10 min)   Discuss the video, asking the participants what strategies for preventing date rape, and abusive relationships in general, were mentioned in the film. (Be sure to emphasize the need for men to clearly have consent.) Ask them to identify gender stereotypes from the film that contribute to abusive relationships.

(25 min)   Role-play and discuss responses to selected coercive or conflict situations seen in the video. This could be done as a full group exercise or in two or three smaller groups with each group being assigned a scenario to role-play for the full group.

SESSION
10

Sexism

GOALS

To examine family and gender role rigidity and its connections to violence

---

SUMMARY OF OBJECTIVES	RESOURCES
I. Check-in II. Recap III. Act Like a Man/Lady IV. Gender Versus Sex V. Define Sexism VI. *Crown Prince* Video	Act Like a Man/Lady Exercises *Crown Prince* video

---

NOTES: _____

_____

_____

_____

_____

_____

_____

_____

_____

_____

SESSION
10

Sexism
Activity Plan

Cofacilitators'
Notes

This session helps us understand that we are not born with masculine/feminine gender roles; rather, these are roles we learn. The Act Like a Man exercise addresses typical defensive reactions when talking about the gender-specific nature of men's violence. It shows why men would go along with their masculine power roles when this is harmful to themselves, their children, and their partners. The Act Like a Lady exercise also demonstrates the pressure put on girls to follow a strict gender code.

These exercises frequently give rise to feelings of male defensiveness among the participants. Expect this and discuss why we feel this. One of the issues will be what psychologists call *cognitive dissonance:* We convince ourselves that we believe in something because it happens to be a part of our lives. Many of us live in very sexist or gender-typed environments (e.g., in our families, in the classroom, at work) and it is difficult for us to hear that these environments may be unhealthy or may foster unhealthy relationships. It may be helpful to emphasize everyone's personal rights and self-autonomy (e.g., just because my father/teacher is abusive/sexist does not mean I need be). Sometimes it also needs to be emphasized that we are not suggesting that "men are bad/abusive" but that gender socialization—both male and female socialization—can lead to unhealthy views of men and women.

The *Crown Prince* video is a fairly powerful dramatization of wife assault and its effect on each family member. Again, keep in mind that some of your participants may have experienced or witnessed woman abuse in their homes, and be sensitive to their needs by allowing them to leave the room, providing an opportunity to speak with you separately, encouraging them to make an appointment with their social worker or a guidance counselor at school, and so on.

This is quite a full session, so be careful that the exercises do not run over the suggested time frames.

TIME FRAME	ACTIVITIES
(115 program minutes)	

(10 min) I Check in. Ask the youths to report if they have had an opportunity during the past week to use any of the assertiveness skills that we have been practicing in group, that is, using DESC, active listening (paraphrasing, empathy, seeking clarification), and recognizing internal and external affective cues (cues that we or others are angry, happy, sad, and so on).

(10 min) II Recap.

(20 min) III Act Like a Man and Act Like a Lady Exercises (see the Session 10 exercises): The purpose of these exercises is to increase our awareness of gender stereotypes: how we learn them, where they come from, and how they are enforced.

(10 min) IV Discuss the difference between *gender* and *sex* and discuss how sex role stereotypes are linked to men's violence in relationships.

- Boys are taught to be controlling.

- Power imbalance may exist in relationships.

- Boys act out feelings aggressively rather than talk them out.

- Girls may stay in abusive relationships longer if this is seen as the norm or if they interpret controlling behavior (e.g., jealousy) as a sign of love.

(10 min) V Ask participants to define *sexism*. This could be done in pairs and then reported back to the large group. We like to use the following definition: *Sexism is a social system that teaches and encourages men to devalue and look down on women and a social system that teaches and encourages women to devalue and look down on themselves and other women.*

Discuss how sexism affects men and women differently, and how it gets in the way of healthy relationships (both intimate relationships and other relationships: parent-child, teacher-student, boss-employee, and so on). Some youths may react to the definition suggested by giving examples of "reverse sexism." Point out that the definition of sexism identifies it as a social system and ask them to provide examples from material learned earlier that shows the historical and current social power differences between men and women.

(10 min)   Break

(40 min)   VI *Crown Prince* Video: Introduce the video as a film that tells the story of a family with two children, a teenager and a 9-year-old, in which the father is violent toward his wife. Give the participants permission to leave the room if they find any part of the video too disturbing to watch.

(10 min)   Discussion of the video should include the following:

- What are your reactions to the video? What are you feeling? thinking?

- How did the two boys differ in their reactions to their father's violence? Why are there differences?

- How might male stereotypes have contributed to the father's use of violence against his wife? his son?

- How might male stereotypes have contributed to Billy's behavior?

- How are the wife and the children kept in a one-down position? (Refer to the Power and Control wheel in the Session 3 exercises.)

- How might female stereotypes have kept the wife trapped in the relationship?

EXERCISES   Act Like a Man

1. *Read Father/Son Dialogue:*

In this situation, the son is lying on the couch watching TV and the dad comes in angry:

Dad: Turn off the TV! What the hell are you doing? And what the hell is this? (Holds up son's report card.)

Son: It's my report card.

Dad: Your report card eh? Well, if you're so smart, why were you stupid enough to get a D in math?

Son: I did the best I could.

Dad: "D" is the best you could do? You're just stupid!

Son: That's not fair! (Tries to get up to leave. Dad shoves him back into the chair.)

Dad: Don't you talk back to me you little brat! (Son starts to cry.) Oh! Now you're going to cry! (Father shakes his son and hits him with the report card.) You can't even act like a man!!

2. Questions

What were the different forms of abuse that we heard in this situation?

The last thing that Dad said before he left the room was, "act like a man." Let's talk about that.

Ask the men in the room to pretend for a moment: You are 10 years old and there is an adult man—father, stepfather, coach, and so on—who is angrily saying to you, "Act like a man." Even if this has not happened to us directly, we have likely seen someone being told to act like a man. Women in the room have also probably heard this statement being made and so all of us have ideas about what it means.

a. What are you learning when someone says that to you (i.e., be tough, don't cry, and so on)?

[Cofacilitator makes a list and places box around the items.]

- All boys learn this as they grow up.
- Taught by whom (parents, friends, teachers, media)?

b. What names are boys called when they try to step outside of this box? [These are listed on the left side of the box under the heading: "Things Said."]

c. What is *the purpose* of these names? What are you supposed to do when someone calls you these names? (e.g., for "fag," the message is you can't be close to other boys or men; being gay is bad). These names are *like little slaps* in the face, telling us to get back into the box. They are emotionally violent, hurt us, and make us want to change so as not to be called them again.

d. What happens to boys *physically*? How are they treated physically to make sure they "act like men"? [These are listed on the right side of the box with the heading: "Things Done."]

So we see that boys are *not born to be* violent but are emotionally and physically hurt to stay in control.

Also note that some of the names boys are called to keep them "in the box" are the names of other nonpower groups (e.g., girl, fag, woman). This further degrades the nonpower group by indicating that to be like them is a bad thing. It also reinforces messages about what men should be and that male attributes are valued and nonpower group attributes are not.

Illustration

Act Like a Man

Things Said	don't show emotion	Things Done
fag	be smart	(physically)
queer	be in control	beat up
sissy	be strong (physically)	bullied
wimp	live up to standards	harassed
girl	rough/tough	isolated
wuss	protectors	ignored
suck	be brave	teased
	don't back down	
	provider	

Act Like a Lady

1. Read Mother/Daughter Dialogue:

In this situation, the daughter is getting ready for a family reunion. She comes out of her room wearing pants and a shirt. Her mother is downstairs wearing a dress.

Mother: You're not wearing that!

Daughter: What's wrong? I'm not wearing jeans!

Mother: What are people going to think? You're going to be meeting people you haven't seen in years and they're going to think you're a tomboy!

Daughter: Mom! I don't care what people think. And I don't want to wear a dress today. You said there might be a baseball game and I can't play baseball in a dress!

Mother: Well I don't care what you think! I will not have people thinking I've raised a tomboy. Go back to your room and change immediately! For goodness sakes, why can't you learn to act like a lady!

As in the Act Like a Man exercise, the same kind of painful, negative training happens for women. There are all kinds of messages about how you should act if you're a "good girl."

2. Questions

What kind of messages is the daughter learning about how she should behave?

What kind of messages is the daughter learning about the importance of her physical appearance?

What kind of messages is the daughter learning about the value of other people's opinions relative to her own?

Where do you think the mother learned these messages?

How is a "lady" or a "good girl" supposed to act? [Cofacilitator draws a flower and lists the teens' ideas inside the flower.]

Like the Act Like a Man box, women are called names to stay in the flower. What names do women get called if they step out of the flower? [Cofacilitator lists these names all around the flower.]

Notice how women are called different names than men. Men get called names about being tough. What do you notice most about the names women are called? (Women are generally identified through the way how they *look,* their sexuality.)

Illustration

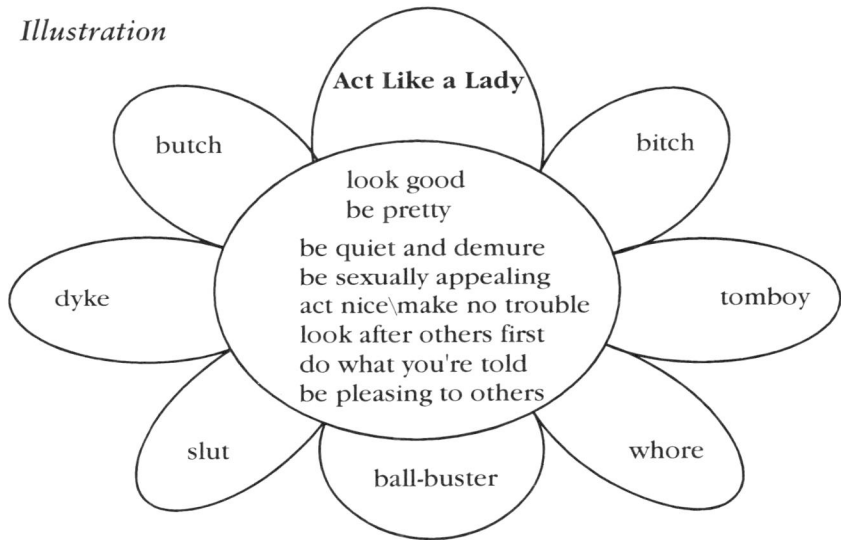

(SOURCE: From *Teens Need Teens: A Manual for Adults Helping Teens Stop Violence,* Creighton & Kivel, 1990. Used with permission.)

SESSION
11

Media and Sexism

NOTES: _____

_____

_____

_____

_____

_____

_____

_____

SESSION
11

Media and Sexism
Activity Plan

The talk show exercise reviews information about violence and provides an opportunity to use skills to respond to negative attitudes. This is an entertaining exercise during which teens enjoy performing for the camera in the position of "experts."

Today's session also focuses on the media as one of the sources from which we learn sexism and gender role rigidity. A short 15-minute clip from the video *Dreamworlds* is used as part of this session. This video tends to elicit stronger reactions from the teens than other videos. *It is extremely important that cofacilitators view this video at least once before the session and read the material we have prepared as a discussion guide.* The following points may also be of some use.

A sense of fairness is important to teens. Therefore, they may struggle with the notion that women do not have equal status with men in our society and that this is reflected in the media (including rock videos). It may be argued by the group that men are seen topless and acting sexually in videos and advertising as much as women. An essential concept to convey is that one image alone is not problematic (i.e., a scantily dressed woman or man). It is the system of images and beliefs that these are tied to that makes them dangerous. During the discussion of the video clip, it may be helpful to refer back to earlier discussions of power imbalance and negative stereotypes to see how these are reinforced. It may also be helpful to show a negative video and a positive one to learn the difference.

TIME FRAME	ACTIVITIES
(120 program minutes)	

(10 min)   I   Check in. Ask members to include examples of sexist stereotypes they encountered during the week in television and movies and among peers, family, and so on.

(10 min)   II   Recap.

(30 min)   III   Create a Talk Show: Participants get involved in an activity that helps rehearse and reinforce prosocial attitudes and behaviors. The activity begins to inoculate participants against proviolent attitudes that they will encounter with others in their peer group. Some optional activities are listed below. The sleazy talk show host exercise has been found to be the most lively and effective. You may wish to provide the youths with the questions or issues in advance and allow them 10 or 15 minutes to prepare their responses. The questions/issues could be divided among smaller groups of two or three participants. Youth often enjoy having this exercise videotaped and then played back at the break.

Some Options:

     A. Produce a teen documentary video with teens interviewing one another about issues that have been discussed (e.g., myths).

     B. Controversial or Sleazy Talk Show: One facilitator can play a sleazy talk show host "looking for the dirt" and arguments. The other facilitator represents all the myths and plays a really negative, obnoxious, and misinformed "expert" (Dr. Brutal). The teens make up a panel of "experts" and provide the prosocial, accurate responses.

Sample issues that could be discussed in either of the above formats include the following "myths":

- The issue of woman abuse is exaggerated; there are just as many women who abuse men.

- If the abuse is so bad, why doesn't the woman just leave the guy?

- Women usually provoke the abuse by their constant nagging.

- A lot of women who cry "rape" are teases who changed their minds.

- A prostitute cannot be raped.

(10 min)   Break

(10 min)   IV   Sources of Gender Stereotypes: Introduce this discussion by asking participants to recap from previous sessions what some of the gender stereotypes are for men and women.

Brainstorm a list of where we learn what it means to be men and women. Point out that some of these sources of learning are unaware of their negative impact (e.g., some friends, adults in our lives). Others quite deliberately target us (e.g., media, advertising). During this discussion, tell the youth that we will now turn to the media to look at its role in the propagation of sexism and violence.

• For example, in the early 1990s, 55% of all rock videos are considered to be sexist, an increase from 45% in 1988. In 95% of those clips, women were portrayed in submissive or sexually suggestive roles (Baby, Chéné, & Dudas, 1992).

(15 min)   V   *Dreamworlds* Video Clip: Introduce the video by commenting that one source of learning gender stereotypes is music videos. Participants will see a video that decodes videos to show how they deliberately send specific messages about what it means to be a man or a woman. Ask the participants to think about how these messages could lead to unhealthy views of men and women.

Cofacilitator Note: Before viewing the video clip, let youths know it is powerful and disturbing. This video requires maturity and consideration of those around them. Because this is a challenging, explicit, and complex video, we recommend that only the introduction and the segment titled, "Ways of Looking: The Gaze and Objectification," be shown during group.

(15 min)   Discussion of video clip to include the following:

• How did you feel while watching the video?

• How were women's roles in the videos portrayed?

• What messages did the videos give about women? about men? Who has more power?

• What is dangerous about these messages?

• It might be said that the women in the video are reduced to objects. What do you think this means?

• What techniques did the videos use to objectify the women?

• What did the video identify as the effects on the real world?

Answers to the above questions and related discussion material are provided (see the Session 11 exercises).

(20 min)   VI   Decode Magazines: Ask participants to break into small groups or pairs and look through magazines for both negative and

positive messages in advertising and photography. It works well to provide each group with a large piece of Bristol board. Divide the Bristol board in half with a marker, and label one side "Positive Images of Women and Men in the Media" and label the other side "Negative Images of Women and Men in the Media." Have the groups paste their images on the paper.

Let the groups know that they will be presenting their posters at group next week. For each example, they will be asked to do the following:

a. Describe the image that you see. Deconstruct the different "ways of looking" (camera angles, body positioning, and so on). What are the advertisers using to sell things?

b. Decode these images to see what they are portraying to be glamorous when we know it is not. What are the negative messages/effects?

Homework: Watch for negative images in songs, videos, television shows, and so on. What are the messages behind the humor or tune? What images are they using? Bring an example of this to the next meeting.

EXERCISES

Dreamworlds: The Realm of Music Videos

We live in a society in which we learn about ourselves from images that promote a few viewpoints while devaluing the rest. A powerful source of these images is music videos. These videos began when advertisers joined together with music producers to reproduce the techniques of advertising in videos. These techniques are very effective in reaching their intended audience. *The following information shows the techniques designed to grab and hold the viewer's attention.*

Definitions: To discuss the effects of sexist images, the terms *objectivity* and *subjectivity* are often used. For this purpose:

1. *Subjectivity* refers to the personality, the presence of thoughts, feelings, and an inner *self*. You see the person as an individual, a human being with likes and dislikes.

2. *Objectivity* refers to the outward appearance only and does not include thoughts, feelings, or personality. A person is seen as a thing (like an object) like many other things. There are no characteristics or emotional attachment.

Purpose of Looking

- All the people in the "Dream" world are to be looked at.
- It's women who are looked at most often:
  —It feels good to watch good-looking women.
  —All the women wear as little clothing as possible.

- How are women watched in the "Dream" world?
  —Women have one purpose: to be objects of desire.
  —Anything the women may be doing is secondary to being looked at.

Ways of Looking: The Gaze and Objectification

These are the untrue laws that govern the women in the "Dream" world:

- Women love being looked at:
  —Women act as if the cameras are always on them. They pose seductively, inviting the constant gaze.
- When women are looking:
  —We don't see through *their* eyes. We don't see what they watch.
- Women's viewpoints are portrayed as unimportant:
  —They are advertising commodities; they are objects to be watched.

We must remember that there is always more than one way to look at something or someone.

Consequences of Looking: The System of Beliefs

- No one image by itself is either good or bad. It's how it ties into a system of beliefs that support sexist stereotyping.
  —For example, a topless man and a topless woman are *not* viewed equally by society. If a man appears topless in public, he is hot. If a woman appears topless, she is a criminal.
- The danger is that the images found in the "Dream" world are presented as reality.
  —Women always want male stares and attention.
  —All women must conform to certain body ideals—thin with large breasts.
  —Women are simply attractive mannequins, passive objects to be used.
  —Women often react passively to men's actions. For example, men touch, position, draw on, and dump water/paint on the women's bodies.
- All the women in the "Dream" world lack subjectivity.
  —The camera travels up and down the women's bodies, slowly emphasizing their curves.
- Underneath shots are "looking up the dress" shots.
  —Women climb up stairs or on ladders.

—Women sit on bar stools or chairs.

- Some shots focus on one part of women's bodies.
  —legs-only shots

  —breasts and hips only

  —"through the standing legs" shot framing the action of performers

- Silhouette shots show women as dark forms with no individual characteristics.
  —We can't tell what the women look like other than the shape of their bodies.

- Some shots interchange one woman for another.
  —Different women are used but the shots are the same.

Are Men and Women Viewed Equally in the "Dream" World?

- Women in the "Dream" world lack subjectivity. The men do not.
  —Even if men appear in the "Dream" world unclothed, they rarely appear "dissected"; their body parts are frequently topped by a face.

- For male performers, the consumer product is the music. Females are sold by their sexual attractiveness.
  —It is not necessary for male musicians to be "drop-dead" gorgeous to "make" it in the music business. For female musicians, it's almost part of the contract to at least be "inoffensive" looking.

- Good-looking men and women are not viewed in the same way in the "Dream" world.
  —Even though men may appear unclothed, they are not passive objects. The men still take action in the "Dream" world. They go after what they want.

- To use women is a socially sanctioned activity. To use men in the same way is not to be tolerated.
  —For example, if a female performer such as Madonna objectifies men in her videos, she leaves herself open to media-induced questions about her morality and personal "appetites." For her to copy the male privilege of objectifying others, she is branded a "slut." For male performers such as David Lee Roth, morality is not subject to such bashing.

- Men are real people in the "Dream" world. Women are not.
  —Focusing on one part of women—namely, their bodies— detracts from thinking about them as real people.

  —The women do not have their own feelings, intellects, dreams, and ambitions.

Conclusion

Nothing is portrayed as unique about the women in the "Dream" world. Nothing depicts them as *real* individuals. They are all essentially the same and are interchangeable. We as viewers are to believe that nothing inside matters, only the body parts have to conform to the conventions of attractiveness. *It is this objectification of women that minimizes the seriousness of such negative behavior as sexual assault.*

Making a Difference
Working Toward Breaking the Cycle of Violence

In this final section, seven sessions are devoted to providing young people with opportunities to do larger scale social action against intimate violence. Up to this point, social action was facilitated within the group and encouraged outside the group, but not set as part of the explicit program agenda. These sessions aim at violence-specific skill building such as confronting sexism, accessing community resources when violence is an issue in teens' lives, and doing a social action event for an antiviolence cause. In other words, we are challenging youths to "go public" with their knowledge about intimate violence and their commitment to positive change.

We hope that these activities will facilitate a sense of group accomplishment as well as substantial individual growth. It is intended that through these various experiences with the community-at-large, the youths will feel a greater sense of empowerment to deal effectively with violence in their own lives as well as to believe in their effectiveness at making a contribution and a difference to the cause of ending intimate violence. Knowing that they can make choices for themselves, some perhaps very different than their friends' or families', would seem an important stepping stone to a nonviolent future. It is in this context of individual and group positive growth that the final session contains a celebration and conclusion to the Youth Relationships Program. After the 18-session program, the youths are invited to continue group support meetings and to stay involved with the Youth Relationships Project. Thus, the approach to the conclusion of the program is, "Thanks, and stay tuned . . ."

SESSION
12

Confronting Sexism and
Violence Against Women

GOALS	To practice responses to sexist comments To learn appropriate responses to peer pressure To learn about community help agencies for problem situations

SUMMARY OF OBJECTIVES	RESOURCES
I. Check-in II. Recap III. Magazine Decoding IV. Responding to Peer Pressure V. Problem Scenarios	Peer pressure scenarios Problem scenarios Problem Scenario Worksheet Telephone books Brochures from community agencies

NOTES: _____

_____

_____

_____

_____

_____

_____

_____

SESSION
12

Confronting Sexism and Violence Against Women
Activity Plan

During this session, participants will rehearse ways of responding to sexist comments and behavior through role-plays. Generally it is helpful if the facilitator plays the role of the character making the sexist remarks while the youths play the prosocial roles. This allows the youths to practice prosocial rather than sexist responses. Note that the first attempt at this work is quite difficult for some participants. A great deal of encouragement and practice are needed.

From this session onward, anytime a sexist comment is made during the group, teens should confront the person who made the comment in an appropriate manner. If this does not occur naturally, and it appears that the comment will slip by unaddressed, the facilitators should stop the group and ask the youths to address the comment by role-playing what an appropriate response would be. An effective way of doing this is to ask the person who was the recipient of the comment how he or she felt when hearing the comment and what he or she might need to hear from the person who made the comment to be comfortable with the resolution of the situation. Sometimes it is appropriate to use the DESC script in response to sexist comments made during the group.

The last exercise in this session involves a problem-solving situation in which the youths are asked to resolve a problem as a couple "team." It is important that cofacilitators pair off the participants so that mature, responsible teens are matched with those who may need more support. Youths typically do not know where to seek help. Beginning with a phone book, the most accessible resource available to teens, it becomes clear that simply knowing how to find social services is problematic. It is surprising how few think of the emergency numbers in the front of the phone book. Facilitators need to be close at hand to provide support. Contacting the agencies is also difficult for many youth. Some teens have felt angry or frustrated about responses they have received from a service agency. Their shyness, nervousness, or giggling has been interpreted as a prank and not taken seriously by the receptionist at the service agency. This indicates an important barrier to teens accessing services. When agencies are not sensitive to the awkwardness and anxious giggling that may accompany teens seeking help, important resources become inaccessible to them.

Cofacilitator preparation for this session includes contacting the agencies that the youths will be calling to ensure their willingness and availability to have the participants come for an agency visit. When contacting the agencies, you should provide a time frame for when the teens will be scheduling the agency visit.

TIME FRAME	ACTIVITIES
(110 program minutes)	

(10 min) I Check in and discuss homework: Ask teens to report back any negative images they saw during the past week in the media and describe what the message was.

(10 min) II Recap.

(15 min) III Magazine Decoding: Report back to the large group the magazine decoding that was completed last session.

(25 min) IV Responding to Peer Pressure: Comment that we have all been in uncomfortable situations where sexist remarks or behavior was a problem, and we felt powerless to act because of the effects of peer pressure (ask the group to think back to the locker room scene in the *Date Rape* video as an example). Ask the participants to give an example of a peer pressure situation that happened to them or someone they know where sexist remarks or behaviors were tolerated because no one felt comfortable addressing them. If the youths do not volunteer a scenario, use the scenarios provided (see the Session 12 exercises).

Discussion Questions:

- Why is it tough to respond to and confront sexist remarks? (For example, you may run the risk of encountering harsh responses; recall the Act Like a Man/Lady exercise.)

- How do you decide when it's worth it to say anything or not? (Sometimes it may be best simply to walk away.)

- How do we respond without being abusive ourselves?

Remind the youths that each time someone confronts negative attitudes, she or he is promoting positive social change. It is much more difficult to go against a group than to go along with a crowd. Even though people may call you a "wimp," you are showing greater strength of character.

Possible Responses to Negative Attitudes:

- "You might think it's stupid, but what you just did contributes to sexism and violence in our society."

- "When people say things like that, I get offended because it is a real put-down to women."

- Walk away or take another action that communicates disapproval.

- "How would you feel if that happened to you?"

Role-play appropriate responses to the situation(s) provided by the youth and/or the scenarios (see the Session 12 exercises). This can be done as a full group or in smaller groups and presented back to the full group.

(10 min)   Break

(40 min)   Problem scenario exercise to be completed in pairs:

1. Each "couple" team is given a problem scenario (see the Session 12 exercises) and told that their assignment for the next few sessions will be to come up with a solution to this situation. They will be given a worksheet to work through, will interview someone at a local community agency, and will gather research on other community agencies from brochures.

2. Meet with each team individually to get them started on the worksheet provided (see the Session 12 exercises). You should also provide each team with a telephone book. Initially, this is the only resource that they are given. Ask them to check with you when they have completed items 1 through 5 on the worksheet. Tell them that they have approximately 10 minutes to complete these items.

3. Once the team reaches item 6, check the following:

- Have they accurately identified what the three most important issues are?

- Have they identified the most appropriate agencies to call? Were they able to locate their telephone numbers?

- Did they place an asterisk beside the name of the agency that is most pivotal to their scenario? (This will be the agency that the team will visit.)

If the central service was not identified, the team is provided with the name and number of the agency. Facilitators have previously contacted these agencies to seek involvement so that calls from teens will be expected (appointment times are usually set as well and are best scheduled after school).

4. Give the teams another 10 minutes to prepare questions to ask at the agency visit. They should use the handout provided (see the Session 12 exercises). Tell them to let you know when they have completed this so that you can practice an agency phone call with them.

5. Role-play the telephone contact with the agencies during which the teens will set up an appointment for an agency visit. The youths may need to write on a piece of paper a script of what they want to say (e.g., "Hello, my name is _____. I am calling from the Youth Relationships Project. . . . As part of this project, we would like to visit your agency to find out more about the services it offers. . . . Would two of us be able to come for an agency visit some time after school next week? . . . What bus do I need to take in order to get there? . . .). (The actual phone calls can be made now or at the start of the next session.)

EXERCISES

Peer Pressure Scenarios

Situation 1

Adam is standing with four of his friends outside the cafeteria at school. Rachel passes by the five guys to go into the cafeteria. "Now there's a nice piece of flesh," says Josh, one of Adam's friends. All the guys laugh and a couple of them whistle at Rachel, who just keeps on walking but looks embarrassed. Adam laughs too, although he notices a tight feeling in his stomach and secretly is feeling bad for Rachel, whom they had obviously embarrassed and intimidated.

Situation 2

Cindy is sitting with her friends in the cafeteria. Several tables away they notice Megan talking and laughing with a bunch of guys, one of whom Cindy likes. Cindy says, "Would you look at Megan . . . she's such a slut . . . that's the only reason guys like her—they think she's easy." Colleen, one of Cindy's friends, thinks to herself that she knows that Megan is no more sexually active than Cindy, but no one else says anything to stick up for Megan so Colleen doesn't either.

Situation 3

Josh and his friends are in the smoking pit just outside the school yard when they see Jason coming from home economics class. Josh yells, "Hey girlie-boy, did you bake us some muffins today?" Everyone laughs. Although Mike laughs the hardest, he secretly feels embarrassed for Jason and worries that the guys will find out that he, like Jason, enjoys cooking and is known among his family members to be a really great cook.

Scenario 1: Narissa and Bill

Narissa: — 16 years old
— lives at home with her parents
— is in Grade 11

Bill: — 17 years old
— lives at home with his mother (parents separated when he was 10 years old)
— is in Grade 12

Bill and Narissa have been dating for about 6 months. Although they have a lot of fun together, sometimes Narissa is worried about Bill's attitude. There are times when he gets very jealous, especially if he sees her talking to other guys. He always asks her to explain where she was and whom she was with when he is not with her. Recently, on a few occasions, he has really yelled at her and called her some horrible names because he thought she was fooling around on him.

The latest crisis occurs after Narissa finds out that she is pregnant. She tells Bill that she is 7 weeks pregnant. At first, Bill denies that the baby is his (although Narissa has not been seeing anyone else). Then he gets really angry with Narissa; he calls her an ignorant slut and tells her that if she wasn't so stupid she wouldn't have gotten pregnant. The two of them start arguing about whose fault it is that Narissa is pregnant. The argument leads to pushing and shoving. Eventually, Bill shoves Narissa and she falls over a coffee table. She holds her stomach and begins crying and saying that Bill might have hurt the baby. Bill starts crying too and says he doesn't know why he gets so out of control. Narissa suggests that he needs help and if he wants she will go with him to try to get help. Bill, who is afraid that one day he may really hurt Narissa or the baby, decides to try to get help for himself.

Scenario 2: Nancy and Bob

Nancy:
— 16 years old
— dropped out of Grade 10 when she was 6 months pregnant
— left home and moved into an apartment with her boyfriend Bob after their son was born
— takes care of their 6-month-old son Robert full time but would like to return to school as soon as possible

Bob:
— 18 years old
— quit school before finishing Grade 12 to support his new family
— works as a construction worker but doesn't really like the job
— left home at the time of his son's birth to move in together with Nancy and Robert

Nancy and Bob are finding parenthood very stressful. They miss their freedom and are finding it difficult to adjust to their new responsibilities. When they argue, which they do often, Bob usually blames Nancy for having gotten pregnant in the first place. They don't have much money and Bob sometimes drinks too much.

The baby has been sick and crying all day. Nancy is frustrated and at her wit's end not knowing what to do with the baby to make it stop crying. Bob has had a long hard day at work, which he doesn't like, but it's the only job he can get. Bob just wants to relax and have a beer, but Nancy gives him the baby and says, "Here, you do something with him. I've had him all day." Bob replies, "That's your job!" and the argument escalates to yelling and throwing things and he eventually slaps her. The neighbors call the police.

Scenario 3a: Carol, Jan, and Linda

Carol:
— 24 years old
— has been employed as a lawyer for 1 year
— lesbian woman with support of family and friends
— has a 3-year-old daughter

Jan:
— 23 years old
— works in assembly at Ford Motors
— has not told others she is lesbian

Linda:
— 24 years old
— a mutual friend of Carol and Jan
— works as a receptionist in an accounting firm

Carol and Jan are in a 3-year relationship and have been living together with Carol's daughter for 2 years. All of Carol's family and friends know she is lesbian and she has a lot of support. Jan has told only two very close friends she is a lesbian, and she fears that her family would not be supportive if they knew. She has told her family that she and Carol are roommates and very good friends. In the past 2 years, Carol has been less tolerant of Jan and has slapped and shoved her on two occasions. On a number of occasions when she has been angry, Carol has threatened to call Jan's parents or her brother and tell them that she and Jan are lovers. Carol often drops little hints when they are visiting Jan's family and Jan fears they may catch on one of these times. Carol only laughs and tells Jan to relax before she just tells them once and for all.

Sometimes Jan thinks she is just overreacting. Carol often tells her she is just being stupid and sometimes calls her worse names. Jan had thought about going back to school but Carol told her that she could never make it even though she had great grades in high school.

Last week, Jan told Carol she was going to go back to school and showed her the application. Carol said they could not afford it and that it would be a waste of money. When Jan said she was determined to find a way, Carol was enraged. She ripped up the application form and threw it in Jan's face. She slapped and punched Jan several times and pushed her down. Carol left the house angry.

Jan needed help but was afraid to tell anyone. She felt isolated because she could not tell her family and was afraid that her and Carol's friends might not believe her. Jan does not want to go to a shelter for abused women and she loves Carol and wants things to work out. A week later, she finally called Linda, who was a very close mutual friend of both Jan and Carol. Linda was very worried when she heard the details on the phone. She said she had been afraid to ask, but had thought for a while that Carol was abusing Jan. Linda came over right away.

Scenario 3b: Joyce, Barb, and Anne

Joyce:
— 17 years old
— Grade 11
— going out with Jeff for 8 months

Barb:
— 16 years old
— Grade 11
— going out with Todd for a year and a half
— 3 months pregnant

Anne:
— 16 years old
— Grade 11
— broke up with John 2 months ago

Joyce, Anne, and Barb have been close friends all through high school. Since Barb has been going out with Todd, Anne and Joyce have not seen a lot of her. When they do get together, Barb tells them that she has to lie to Todd about where she is because he doesn't like her going out with anyone without him there. In fact, for the past 6 months, Barb says Todd has been acting really jealous. He calls her a tramp or worse and says she is looking at other guys when she is not. Sometimes he pushes her around, and he slapped her once. Barb is afraid that Todd may really hurt her and would break up with him but she is afraid. In addition, she says he had a rough childhood and needs her. She is very confused; she thinks Todd must really love her because he gets so jealous.

Anne said she broke up with her boyfriend, John, 2 months ago because he was acting really jealous and started telling her what to do. She really liked him but told him she did not want to be treated like that. The next time he did it, she ended the relationship. She misses him a lot but is glad she did not wait any longer, especially after hearing what Barb is going through.

Joyce said she and Jeff have a good relationship. He makes her feel good about herself and says he does not like the way some of his friends talk about girls and their own girlfriends. Joyce and Jeff make decisions together and agree to also have their own friends. When they have an argument, they talk about how they are feeling and try to understand each other's position. Sometimes they wait until the next day to discuss the problem, but they always do discuss it. Joyce says Jeff really respects her.

Barb says she would like to leave her relationship like Anne did and to be in a relationship like Joyce has, but she has tried to leave and feels she can't. Once, Todd threatened to kill himself if she ever left him and she thinks he just might! Barb says she would like to see a counselor who knows about these things but does not think she needs to go to the women's shelter. She also said she would go if Joyce and Anne came with her for the first visit.

Scenario 4: Ken, Jackie, and Dan

Jackie: — 17 years old
— Grade 12
— experienced date rape

Ken: — 17 years old
— Grade 12
— grew up with Jackie, lives a few doors down, close friends, wants to help

Dan: — raped Jackie
— 18 years old, popular in school
— final year of high school

Ken ran into Jackie sitting in the park near their homes on the way back from school. She just seemed to be staring off into space and she had not been at school the past 2 days (it is now Tuesday). When Ken sat down next to her and said, "Hi!" Jackie jumped and after she saw it was only Ken she started crying. Ken said he was sorry, that he didn't mean to scare her. She said it was not that, she said something bad had happened after the party on Friday night. Ken got worried and asked what happened.

Jackie explained that after the party, Dan invited her back to his place because his parents were away and he was having some people over. Jackie said she liked Dan and had wanted to go out with him for a long time. When they got to Dan's place, no one else was there. Jackie accepted a drink that Dan offered her, even though she had too much to drink already.

Before long, Dan was pushing her to go into the bedroom with him but Jackie said no. He kept bugging her, saying that he knew she had sex with other guys, so what was wrong with him. Jackie said she liked him but that she did not want to have sex. Dan called her names and when she got up to leave, he pushed her onto the couch and started kissing her. He was touching her and then forced himself on her. Jackie did not know what to say anymore or how to stop him. She was frozen until it was all over and Dan took her home.

Ken wanted to call the police right away, but Jackie did not want to. She felt it was her fault because she did sleep with another guy that she liked—even though it was when *she* wanted to. She felt guilty because Dan had said he knew she really wanted sex because of the sleazy dress she was wearing. Jackie also said she was drinking too much and that she should have known better.

Ken could see Jackie was still really shaken up by the situation. She had not eaten or slept much since it happened and was afraid to go to school because Dan was so popular and probably had told all the other guys by now. She was also afraid to face him and did not trust being around other guys. Ken was the only person she could talk to.

Scenario 5: Ali and Mobina

Ali:
— 27 years old
— an architectural engineer
— born in India
— emigrated to Canada at age 12 with his parents

Mobina:
— 27 years old
— does not work outside the home
— born in Canada although her parents were born in India

John:
— 5 years old

Muira:
— 4 years old

Ali and Mobina have been married for 6 years. When they married at age 21, they were both in their second year at the university. Mobina dropped out of the university at the beginning of her third year to stay home and care for their first child, John. Although she had mixed feelings about doing this, Ali felt very strongly that a mother should be at home with her children. So Mobina quit school after the birth of John while Ali completed his engineering degree.

Although Mobina enjoyed caring for her children, as the years passed she became more and more regretful that she had not finished her economics degree. Mobina really wanted to work in her chosen field of study. This too became a topic about which Ali and Mobina argued a great deal. Ali did not want Mobina to work outside the home; he felt that it was not necessary because he made a good salary. In fact, Ali worried that his family and their Indian friends would think that he was a poor provider if his wife went out and worked—it would be an embarrassment to him.

Once both John and Muira were in school, Mobina began to pressure Ali more to allow her to go back to the university so that she could finish her degree and possibly work as an economist. Ali and Mobina found themselves arguing more and more, about Mobina returning to school and many other family matters including raising the children (Ali thought that Mobina was not strict enough and did not spend enough time with them) and problems with each other's in-laws. Mobina felt that Ali's family was very critical about how she raised the children, and they sided with Ali in their arguments about Mobina going to back to school and working. The arguments between Ali and Mobina became more and more heated until one day Ali hit Mobina repeatedly with a rolled up newspaper he had been holding. Although Mobina was not seriously injured, she was both shocked and humiliated, not only because her husband had done this but also because the beating had occurred in front of their two small children. Ali as well was shocked by what he had done and told Mobina over and over again how sorry he was. He promised that it would never happen again.

Problem Scenario Worksheet: Getting Help!

Problem situation (summarize in your own words):

_____

_____

_____

_____

Given the detailed problem situation above, please list all of the problems and issues this couple is facing.

_____

_____

_____

_____

What are the main problems that they must work on?

_____

_____

_____

_____

Think about where you could get help both together and/or separately . . .

_____

_____

_____

_____

How would you find the services you need?

_____

_____

_____

_____

What will it cost?

_____

_____

_____

_____

What is involved?

_____

_____

_____

_____

List below at least six agencies or services that you could go to for help if you were in this problem situation.

Agencies/Community Support

	AGENCY	PHONE NUMBER
1.		
2.		
3.		
4.		
5.		
6.		

Now you will choose one of the agencies you selected above and you will call to make an appointment to visit that agency.

On the next page is a data sheet for you to come up with six questions to ask in your interview. You may even want to role-play your situation with them (really pretend you are that person).

When you call the agency, tell them you are from the Youth Relationships Project. They are expecting your call.

At the meeting following your agency visit, you will present to the group what you learned so that all of us can learn about what kind of help is available for ourselves and our friends.

Agency Information

Name of agency: _____

Address: _____

Contact person: _____ Phone number: _____

Questions

1. _____
   _____
   _____
   _____

2. _____
   _____
   _____
   _____

3. _____
   _____
   _____
   _____

4. _____
   _____
   _____
   _____

5. _____
   _____
   _____
   _____

6. _____
   _____
   _____
   _____

Agency Visit

Answers and Additional Information

1. _____
   _____
   _____
   _____

2. _____
   _____
   _____
   _____

3. _____
   _____
   _____
   _____

4. _____
   _____
   _____
   _____

5. _____
   _____
   _____
   _____

6. _____
   _____
   _____
   _____

_____

Contact Person: Signature

Getting to Know Community Helpers for Relationship Violence

GOALS   To continue planning for community agency visits
               To talk about social action

SUMMARY OF OBJECTIVES

I. Check-in
II. Recap
III. Phone Calls to Agencies
IV. Presenting Team Plans
V. Making Changes
VI. Planning Social Action

NOTES: _____

_____

_____

_____

_____

_____

_____

_____

_____

_____

SESSION
13

Getting to Know Community Helpers
for Relationship Violence
Activity Plan

Cofacilitator's
Notes
Today's session continues planning for the agency visit and intro-duces the teens to the idea of planning a social action. Social action can range from a fund-raising event to a letter to the editor. It is important to go with the energy of the group while remaining realistic about what can be done within three to four sessions. A fund-raiser often leaves much work to facilitators (e.g., booking space and alerting media representatives). Some of these arrange-ments need to be made 4 to 6 weeks in advance. This may limit what social action your group will decide to take on. If your group decides on a fund-raiser, they need to choose which charity or agency to raise funds for. It should be one that is involved in preventing woman abuse and/or offering assistance to women who are victims of violence. We have found it to be very rewarding for the group to make the presentation to the charitable recipient.

Cofacilitators should note that although this component of the program involves a fair amount of work, it is considered extremely important to the success of the program because it encourages moral ownership of the principle of nonviolence and because it demonstrates to teens that they actually can make a difference in their community.

TIME FRAME	ACTIVITIES

(110 program minutes)

(10 min)   I   Check in. Ask members to include examples of sexist stereo-types they encountered during the week in TV, movies, among peers, among family, and so on, *or* opportunities that they had during the past week to practice their assertiveness skills.

(10 min)   II   Recap.

(10 min)   III   Make phone calls to arrange agency visits. The visits should occur sometime during the next week. The agency should be expecting the youth's call, based on prior contact from the group facilitator.

(30 min)   IV   Each team plan is presented to the full group. Each team presents their scenario, including the following:

- What they have identified as the major problems

- Which agencies they have identified as important

- Which agency they will visit and when

- What questions they plan to ask of the agency

Participants are encouraged to offer feedback, perhaps making suggestions that the team hadn't thought of regarding resource services or questions to ask the agency.

(10 min)   Break

(20 min)   V   Making Changes: Using the knowledge and skills we all have, brainstorm what we can do as individuals to help end violence against women in our community (e.g., support friends who are in abusive relationships, tell others about available community resources, continue to challenge our own attitudes and those of the people around us).

Then, discuss what we can do as a group to share what we know with others and to end violence against women in the community.

Examples:

- Design a poster

- Produce a video or presentation for use in future groups or local schools

- Produce a drawing, comic, or article for school newspapers

- Get involved in producing an ongoing newsletter with this program about teens against violence

- Organize a fund-raising event for a local organization, such as the women's shelter that works to end violence against women

(25 min) VI Begin to talk about fund-raiser ideas or other social actions that the group will plan. Brainstorm various options (car wash, walk-a-thon, swim-a-thon, raffle, selling chips at a dance, gift wrapping in a mall, organizing a game-day for children at a local women's shelter, and so on).

- Pick one project from the list that was generated.

- If the event is to be a fund-raiser, decide which organization your group would like to raise funds for and contact this organization (they may have brochures or posters that they would like you to display at the event).

- Begin to organize (brainstorm) and assign tasks.

- Some tasks may need to be assigned as homework.

- Attempt to involve local celebrities, athletes, police, politicians, the media, and so on.

- Past group participants could be invited for assistance.

(5 min) VII Organize Participants for the Agency Visit: The participants will be completing their agency visit during the next session. Make sure that the youths leave with the "Agency Information" sheet on which they have recorded the name, address, phone number, and contact person of the agency they are to visit, and the questions they will ask once there. Remind the youths to record the responses to these questions on the answer sheet and to have the contact person sign the sheet. Also make sure that each person has his or her partner's phone number in case they need to contact each other regarding transportation to the agency or any other matter that may arise. Tell the youths to call you (the facilitator) if any problem arises related to the agency visit. (There are usually one or two participants who do not do the agency visit and have some very creative excuses about why they didn't—having them call you if there is a problem helps reduce the chance of this occurrence).

Cofacilitator Note: Watch out for a situation where one youth seems to be doing all the work, especially if the other youth did not go to the agency visit. In this case, it may be helpful to give both youths specific structured tasks. Some teams will complete this exercise quite independently, while others will need your constant feedback and help with structuring the task.

SESSION
14

Getting Out and About in the Community: Visiting Social Service Agencies

---

GOALS	To visit community agencies to build confidence and comfort in using needed services and in supporting peers to do so

SUMMARY OF OBJECTIVES	RESOURCES
I. Agency Visits	Local community agencies

NOTES: _____

_____

_____

_____

_____

_____

_____

_____

_____

_____

_____

Getting Out and About in the Community:
Visiting Social Service Agencies
Activity Plan

Cofacilitators' Notes

Facilitators should be available for phone calls because teens may forget their papers or directions to the agency they are to visit. Although all participants are encouraged to participate in the agency visit, usually at least one member from each team attends the scheduled agency visit. Teams are developed with this in mind, and a mature, responsible teen should be matched with one who may need more support.

Follow-up with the agencies is important because some teens do not show up and people at the agency have set time aside for them. A formal thank you note can be written at the next session.

TIME FRAME
(120 program minutes)

ACTIVITIES

(120 min)   Teams visit identified agencies in the community. The agency visits give the participants practice in identifying and seeking out the services of community supports.

Alternatively, this session may be done as an additional session between regularly scheduled meetings so that two sessions are held in this week.

SESSION
15

Getting Out and About in the Community: Experience at Social Service Agencies

---

GOALS

To share experiences and information gained from agency visits
To make further plans for social action event

SUMMARY OF OBJECTIVES

RESOURCES

I. Check-in
II. Further Research
III. Sharing Information
IV. Thank You Letters
V. Personal Support
VI. Social Action
   Planning
VII. Conclusion
   Planning

Problem Scenario Worksheet

NOTES: _____

_____

_____

_____

_____

_____

Getting Out and About
in the Community
Activity Plan

Cofacilitators' Notes

Youths who complete their agency visits usually find this experience to be very interesting and informative. Call any agency that had no teens show up for the agency visit to apologize and express your appreciation for the time they had set aside to see the youths. Write thank you notes to all the agencies who committed their time to meeting with the youths.

This session also reminds youths that the end of the group is approaching. Conclusion may be difficult for the group. The youths have done a lot of sharing and have likely developed a very special bond. It is important to begin to talk about the approaching conclusion of the group and to allow them the opportunity to express these feelings.

TIME FRAME
(120 program minutes)

ACTIVITIES

(15 min)   I   Check in: In addition to the usual check-in, participants may want to share their experiences from their agency visits.

(20 min)   II   Further Research: "Couple" teams are asked to do further research by looking through pamphlets and making calls to ask questions of other service agencies they did not approach. Each team seeks out relevant information from at least one other agency identified as important on their Problem Scenario

worksheet (see Session 12 exercises). Based on information gathered from agency visits, telephone interviews, and brochures, the teams are asked to develop a solution or plan of action for their problem scenario. This information will be presented to the full group.

(25 min)   III Sharing Information: Encourage participants to give feedback and encourage teams to identify what they might have done differently if confronted with the same situation.

(15 min)   IV Thank You Letters: On a piece of flip chart paper or blackboard, brainstorm a generic thank you letter that can be sent to each of the agencies that the participants visited. Provide the participants with paper (or thank you cards) and stamped envelopes and ask them to write a thank you letter to the agency that they visited. These can be mailed by a cofacilitator after the session.

(10 min)   Break

(5 min)   V Personal Support: Review how this information is important to ending violence at the "personal level." Remind the youths that they now have information to help themselves in the future if they should need it, and information to help family and friends who may need it.

(20 min)   VI Fund-Raiser/Social Action Discussion: Moving back to the bigger picture (the community), continue planning the upcoming social action event.

(10 min)   VII Conclusion: Discuss the approach of the group ending and plan a fun, celebratory activity for the last meeting.

Suggestions:

- A pizza party (with music or a nonviolent video of their choice)

- Bowling

The activity may depend on whether or not your group has a budget to spend on this event.

SESSION
16

Getting Out and About in the Community: Planning for Social Action to End Relationship Violence

GOALS	To learn to support others in problem situations To finish planning for social action event

SUMMARY OF OBJECTIVES	RESOURCES
I. Check-in II. Recap III. Supporting Others IV. Planning Social Action V. Future Social Action	Tips for Helping handout

NOTES: _____

_____

_____

_____

_____

_____

SESSION
16

Getting Out and About in the Community
Activity Plan

An important message to get across about "helping" is that we can provide options for others, but we cannot make them accept our help. To assist an abused woman, we need to know when to call police, what services are available, and how to listen and support without judging. The hard part is not giving up and not imposing our beliefs about what is best. To help an abuser, we need to confront him supportively to make it clear that his behavior is a crime and that he is responsible.

This is the last opportunity to spend group time preparing for the fund-raiser or other social action event. Try to ensure the commitment of the participants in following through with the event. You may choose to invite former group participants to assist in carrying out this event.

TIME FRAME
(120 program minutes)

ACTIVITIES

(10 min) I Check in: Ask members to include examples of sexist stereotypes they encountered during the week in TV, movies, among peers, among family, and so on, *or* opportunities that they had during the past week to practice their assertiveness skills.

(10 min) II Recap.

(10 min)   III Supporting Others:

Begin this discussion by asking the teens how they might feel when someone they know is in an abusive relationship but defends the abuser, refuses to leave, or keeps going back to him.

Acknowledge the validity of the feelings of frustration and helplessness the teens may express, especially now that they are aware of available community resources.

Ask the teens to brainstorm what they could do.

Examples include the following:

- Listening

- Providing information

- Talking to others about the difficulty of being in this situation

- Being patient

Summarize by reminding the teens that consistent and reliable support will probably be the most helpful response, especially for victims of woman abuse, because an abuser will try to keep her isolated and away from her friends and family.

(20 min)   Review the Tips for Helping handout (see the Session 16 exercises). Role-play using these tips by sensitively responding to disclosure of abuse by a friend. Use scenarios from videos viewed thus far (e.g., *Date Rape, Right From the Start*) and/or experiences the youths have disclosed (that happened to them or to someone they know—get a youth's permission first to role-play his or her situation) and/or write an appropriate scenario. This exercise can be done as a full group or in smaller groups, then presented back to the full group.

(10 min)   Break

(40 min)   IV Planning of an event should already be well under way, and this session is dedicated to finalizing arrangements for the fund-raiser or other social action to take place at the next meeting.

- Assign tasks.

- Make confirmation calls.

- Prepare materials (e.g., posters).

- Attend to last-minute details.

- Be sure participants are clear on the date, time, and place of the event and what they are responsible for.

(20 min) V Where Do We Go From Here? Some past group participants have continued to meet on a fairly informal basis so as to stay connected and to plan social action events. This group that continues to meet currently calls itself the Youth Action group. One of the youths takes on the responsibilities of chairperson for the group. Past group facilitators have volunteered to sit in on these meetings and help out with social action events on a rotating basis. The facilitators are primarily there for support. The group is meant to be as youth directed as possible. In addition, some past participants have helped to run future groups as youth cofacilitators, and several youths have become members of the Youth Relationships Project advisory committee.

Brainstorm ideas for maintaining gains made during the program and for continuing to promote ending violence in our community. Cofacilitators may assist with arriving at a list including items such as the following:

- Return to help out with future program groups such as giving an overview of the program to new participants.

- Start a peer support group aimed at ending violence in teen relationships through peer programs in local schools or other agencies.

- Produce a poster or video for future groups or for use in local schools.

- Encourage friends to get involved in a peer support group and contact the program for assistance at any time in the future.

Discuss a teen network against violence. Is there interest in working on strategies to end violence in the community and in the teen culture? Visions: Brainstorm what this might be about.

EXERCISES

Tips for Helping

1. Believe her. Listen to her without judgment.
2. Ask how you can be of most help to her.
3. Encourage her to talk about the assault but *do not* pressure her to talk.
4. Help her to make her own decisions, do not "take over" for her. She needs to regain her sense of control.
5. Recognize your own feelings as separate from hers.

SESSION
17

Getting Out and About in the Community:
Social Action to End Relationship Violence

GOALS   To raise community awareness and/or raise money to help end
                     relationship violence

SUMMARY OF OBJECTIVES

I. Social Action Event

NOTES: _____

_____

_____

_____

_____

_____

_____

_____

_____

_____

_____

_____

SESSION
17

Getting Out and About in the Community Activity Plan

The fund-raiser/social action event could replace this session. However, if there is a shortage of time to complete the program, the event could take place between sessions.

TIME FRAME
(120 program minutes)

SESSION
18

End of Group Celebration

GOALS	To provide a celebration event to youths to reward hard work during group program and to celebrate successful social action

SUMMARY OF OBJECTIVES	RESOURCES
I. Check-in II. Program Evaluation III. Celebration	Group Participant Feedback Form

NOTES: _____

_____

_____

_____

_____

_____

_____

_____

_____

_____

_____

_____

SESSION
18

End of Group Celebration
Activity Plan

Cofacilitators' Notes	The time line provided for this session need not be adhered to. For example, the "fun activity" may require more time than the suggested 80 minutes. In addition, if the fun activity will take place somewhere other than the usual meeting place (e.g., at an amusement park or movie theater), you may wish to schedule separate meeting times for the fun activity and the first two parts of this session (check-in and program evaluation).

TIME FRAME
(120 program minutes)

ACTIVITIES

(20 min) I   Check in: It is important during this final check-in to ask the youths to report how they are feeling about the group ending. This may be a difficult task for the teens that may be eased by having the cofacilitators check in first and disclose their own feelings related to this issue.

(20 min) II   Program Evaluation: Participants complete an evaluation of the group program.

(80 min) III   Celebration: Fun activity such as amusement park, pizza party, movie, bowling (or other youth suggestions).

EXERCISES | Group Participant Feedback Form

Please answer the following questions about your experiences with this group:

I have found this group:

Interesting	1	2	3	4	5	6	7	Not interesting
Informative	1	2	3	4	5	6	7	Not informative

In this group, I have felt:

Bored	1	2	3	4	5	6	7	Not bored
Happy	1	2	3	4	5	6	7	Not happy
Tense	1	2	3	4	5	6	7	Not tense
Calm	1	2	3	4	5	6	7	Not calm
Supported by others	1	2	3	4	5	6	7	Not supported by others
I am a support to the others	1	2	3	4	5	6	7	I am not a support to the others

1. Three important issues that were talked about were:

    _____

    _____

    _____

2. The most useful part of this group was:

    _____

    _____

    _____

3. What I liked best about the group was:

    _____

    _____

    _____

4. What I didn't like about the group was:

    _____

    _____

    _____

APPENDIX A

Alternative Ice-Breaker Exercises

EXERCISES

Option 1: Who Are You?

This exercise requires some preparation by cofacilitators and may only be appropriate if there is quick and easy access to a photocopier.

Briefly interview each teen to gather basic facts about his or her life. A list of potential questions is provided below. Draw up a master list on which you have included one interesting question about each teen. For example, if you find out that Joe has six siblings and that Beth has visited Alaska, you would write on the master list:

- Who has six brothers and sisters?
- Who has been to Alaska?

Once this list is completed, make enough copies for everybody and distribute the question sheet. The teens then go around the room trying to fill in the answers to the questions. For example, a teen might ask the first person if he or she has six brothers and sisters. If the answer is yes, the teen writes down that person's name, and moves on to the next person. To encourage them to meet with each teen several times, the teens are only allowed to ask one question of one person at a time.

Potential Interview Questions

- How many brothers and sisters do you have?
- Where is the farthest place you have visited?
- In which city were you born?
- What sports do you play?
- What was the last movie you saw?
- Have you ever met anyone famous? If so, whom?
- What food do you absolutely hate?

- What's your favorite thing to do on a Saturday morning?
- If you had a million dollars to spend on one thing, what would you buy?
- What is the strangest thing you like to put on top of pizza?
- Have you ever won a trophy or an award? If so, what for?

Option 2: You Did What?!?

Hand out small pieces of paper and ask the teens to think of something strange or unusual that they have done or that has happened to them. It is helpful to give the youth an illustration from the cofacilitators' experiences. Make sure they keep this idea to themselves.

Have the youths write down this experience. As you collect the papers, it's a good idea to check what they have written to ensure the experience is appropriate (i.e., steer teens away from illegal or sexual activities).

Once all the papers are collected, shuffle them, redistribute them, and instruct the teens to find the person who wrote down the experience. Once everyone has found their respective partners, gather back in a circle and have the teens introduce their partners by telling the group about their partners' strange experience.

Note: As with all exercises, it is expected that cofacilitators participate as well.

APPENDIX
B

Forms

Eligibility Form

_____
Office Use

Please complete this form for any youth between the ages of 14 and 16 who has consented to be contacted for involvement in research with the Youth Relationships Project.

Name of Youth: _____ _____
                 Last   First

Address: _____

Date of Birth: _____   Gender: _____   Today's Date: _____
               d/m/y   M/F

Name of Social Worker: _____   Phone: _____

Agency: _____

Is caregiver consent required?   Yes _____   No _____

Please answer the following questions to the best of your knowledge. If uncertain, please indicate.

Does the Above-Named Youth Have:

1. Current or previous involvement with your agency or another child welfare agency?

   Yes _____   No _____
   If so, from _____ (month/year) to _____ (month/year)

2. A history of maltreatment prior to age 12?

   Yes _____ No _____
   [Please complete the information enclosed.]

3. A life-threatening medical illness, chronic disability, neurological illness, or acute injury requiring treatment?

   Yes _____ No _____
   Please describe: _____
   _____

4. A recent psychiatric diagnosis, or is he/she currently under the care of a physician or psychologist for treatment of any psychological disorders?

   Yes _____ No _____
   Please describe: _____
   _____

5. A measured IQ below 75 (test findings in records)?

   Yes _____ No _____

6. Prior incarceration (closed detention) stemming from criminal charges for a crime against persons (e.g., sexual assault, mugging) since age 12?

   Yes _____ No _____

7. The time or schedule available to attend for 18 weeks?

   Yes _____ No _____

8. Prior or current residential treatment or hospitalization for a psychiatric disorder?

   Yes _____ No _____
   Please describe: _____
   _____

9. What is the current status of this youth at your agency (e.g., wardship, supervision order, upcoming placement changes)?

   _____

After receipt of this form, we will contact the youth to arrange for an interview. Please call us if you have questions.

Intake Form

I.D. No.: _____

1. What is your race or ethnic origin?

    _____

2. Are you currently attending school?
    YES   NO
    If yes, name of school: _____
    Grade in school:

3. Do you currently have a full-time or part-time job?   YES   NO
    If yes, employment:_____

4. Whom do you live with? _____

5. Who primarily raised you? _____

6. What is the marital status of your parents?

    _____

7. How many children are in your family?

    _____

8. Father's occupation: _____

9. Mother's occupation: _____

10. Are you involved in extracurricular activities at school or in the community (i.e., drama, music, sports)?

    _____

    _____

11. What do you like to do for fun?

    _____

    _____

12. Have you begun dating?   YES   NO

13. Do you currently have a steady boy/girlfriend?   YES   NO
    If yes, how long have you been seeing each other?

    _____

14. What is the longest relationship you've been in?

    _____

    _____

15. What contact have you had with legal authorities?

    _____

    _____

16. Describe your responsibilities at home (i.e., chores and so on):

    _____

    _____

17. What things do you and your parents argue about?

    _____

    _____

18. What kinds of discipline do your parents currently use?

    _____

    _____

19. Describe your relationship with your parents:

    _____

    _____

20. Describe your relationship with your brothers/sisters:

    _____

    _____

21. Describe your relationship with your friends:

    _____

    _____

22. How often do you meet with your social worker?

_____

_____

23. What CAS services (group programs) have you been involved in?

_____

_____

Participant Rating Form

This form may be completed by facilitators on a weekly basis for each participant. Rate each participant on the following scale:

Very Low   1   2   3   4   5   6   7   Very High

Participant	Self-Expression Skills	Supported by Others	Support Given to Others	Involvement and Participation	Listening Skills	Disruptive Behavior

Definitions for Participant Rating Form

Self-Expression: The youth clearly articulates a position on an issue, own feelings, and/or past experiences in a respectful manner.

Support Received: Other group members verbally or nonverbally indicate empathy and/or understanding toward the youth (e.g., nodding, statement of reinforcement, etc.).

Support Given: The youth verbally or nonverbally indicates empathy and/or understanding toward other youths.

Involvement and Participation: The youth positively contributes to the group process (e.g., contributes to group discussion, attends while others are speaking, participates in role plays, takes a leadership role in small groups, etc.).

Listening: The youth attends while others are speaking.

Disruptive Behavior: The youth displays any verbal or nonverbal behavior that impedes the group process (e.g., creating distractions, inappropriate laughter, off-topic behavior, etc.).

Rating Scale

(7) Very High: Occurs for almost all of the group and/or at very high intensity.

(1) Very Low: Occurs for almost none of the group and/or at very low intensity.

Please note: All of these categories are rated on observed (not inferred) behavior.

References

Babcock, J., Waltz, J., Jacobson, N., & Gottman, J. (1993). Power and violence: The relation between communication patterns, power discrepancies, and domestic violence. *Journal of Consulting and Clinical Psychology, 61,* 40-50.

Baby, F., Chéné, J., & Dudas, H. (1992). *Les femmes dans les vidéoclip: Sexisme et violence.* Québec: Gouvernement de Québec, Étude réalisé pour le Conseil de Statut de la Femme.

Bower, S. A., & Bower, G. H. (1976). *Asserting yourself: A practical guide for positive change.* Reading, MA: Addison-Wesley.

Brown, M. (1994, April 21). Youth voice needs outlet. *London Free Press,* p. B4.

Bussey, K., & Bandura, A. (1992). Self-regulatory mechanisms governing gender devlopment. *Child Development, 63,* 1236-1250.

Carr, R., & Saunders, G. (1981). *Peer counseling starter kit.* Victoria, BC: Peer Systems Consulting Group, Inc.

Creighton, A., & Kivel, P. (1990). *Teens need teens: A manual for adults helping teens stop violence.* Contra Costa County, CA: Battered Women's Alternatives. (Order number: 1-800-266-5592)

Dryfoos, J. G. (1990). *Adolescents at risk: Current prevalence and intervention.* New York: Oxford University Press.

Dutton, D. G. (1995). *The domestic assault of women: Psychological and criminal justice perspectives.* Vancouver: University of British Columbia Press.

Finkelhor, D., Hotaling, G., Lewis, I. A., & Smith, C. (1990). Sexual abuse in a national survey of adult men and women: Prevalence, characteristics, and risk factors. *Child Abuse & Neglect, 14,* 19-28.

Fisher, J. D., & Fisher, W. A. (1992). Changing AIDS risk behavior. *Psychological Bulletin, 111,* 455-474.

Frost-Knappman, E. (1994). *Women's progress in America.* Santa Barbara, CA: ABC-CLIO.

Gelles, R. J., & Straus, M. A. (1988). *Intimate violence.* New York: Simon & Schuster.

Jaffe, P. J., Suderman, M., Reitzel, D., & Killop, S. (1993). *Myths and facts of wife assault: Questionnaire* (unpublished). (Available from London Family Court Clinic, 254 Pall Mall Street, Suite 200, London, Ontario N6A 5P6)

Mahoney, M. J. (1991). *Human change processes.* New York: Basic Books.

Millstein, S. G., Peterson, A. C., & Nightingale, E. O. (1993). *Promoting the health of adolescents: New directions for the twenty-first century.* New York: Oxford University Press.

Olsen, K. (1994). *Chronology of women's history*. Westport, CT: Greenwood.

Ontario Women's Directorate. (1995, March). *Sexual assault: Dispelling the myths*. Toronto: Author.

Pence, E., & Paymar, M. (1993). *Education groups for men who batter: The Duluth model*. New York: Springer.

Pollitt, K. (1991, April 7). The Smurfette principle. *New York Times Magazine*, pp. 22-24.

Sinclair, D. (1985). *Understanding wife assault: A training manual for counselor and advocates*. Toronto: Ministry of Community and Social Services.

Smith, M. J. (1975). *When I say no I feel guilty: How to cope using the skills of systematic assertive therapy*. New York: Dial.

Starr, R., & Wolfe, D. A. (1991). *The effects of child abuse and neglect: Issues and research*. New York: Guilford.

Statistics Canada. (1993). *Violence against women: A national survey*. Hull, Quebec: Author.

Straus, M. A., & Gelles, R. (1990). *Physical violence in American families: Risk factors and adaptations to violence in 8,145 families*. New Brunswick, NJ: Transaction Books.

U.S. Advisory Board on Child Abuse and Neglect. (1990). *Child abuse and neglect: Critical first steps in response to a national emergency* (Stock No. 017-092-00104-5). Washington, DC: Government Printing Office.

U.S. Senate Judiciary Committee. (1992, October). *Violence against women: A week in the life of America* (prepared by the majority staff of the Senate Judiciary Committee). (Available from Hart Office Bldg., Room B04, Washington, DC 20510)

Walker, L. E. A. (1989). Psychology and violence against women. *American Psychologist, 44*, 695-702.

Wekerle, C., & Wolfe, D. A. (1993). Prevention of child physical abuse and neglect: Promising new directions. *Clinical Psychology Review, 13*, 501-540.

Wekerle, C., Wolfe, D. A., & Lefebvre, L. (1995). *History of child maltreatment and adolescent insecure attachment models: The double relationship whammy* (Manuscript under review). Ontario: University of Western Ontario, Department of Psychology.

Willett, J. B., Ayoub, C. C., & Robinson, D. (1991). Using growth modeling to examine systematic differences in growth: An example of change in the functioning of families at risk of maladaptive parenting, child abuse, or neglect. *Journal of Consulting and Clinical Psychology, 59*, 38-47.

Wolfe, D. A. (1994, October). *Perpetrators of violence against women and children: Common themes*. Address presented to the annual convention of the Society for Traumatic Stress Studies, San Antonio, TX.

Wolfe, D. A., Wekerle, C., Gough, R., & Reitzel, D. (1993, August). *Promoting healthy, non-violent relationships: A prevention program for youth*. Paper presented in the symposium titled "Violence in Adolescent Relationships: Identifying Risk Factors and Prevention Methods" (D. Wolfe, Chair), at the 101st annual meeting of the American Psychological Association, Toronto.

Wolfe, D. A., Wekerle, C., McEachran, A., Pittman, A., Reitzel-Jaffe, D., & Grasley, C. (1995). An innovative approach to child abuse prevention: Promoting healthy relationships during adolescence. In D. A. Wolfe, R. McMahon, & R. D. Peters (Eds.), *Child abuse: New directions in prevention and treatment across the lifespan*. Manuscript in preparation.

Wolfe, D. A., Wekerle, C., Reitzel-Jaffe, D., & Gough, R. (1995). Strategies to address violence in the lives of youth. In E. Peled, P. G. Jaffe, & J. L. Edleson (Eds.), *Ending the cycle of violence: Community responses to children of battered women* (pp. 255-274). Thousand Oaks, CA: Sage.

Wolfe, D. A., Wekerle, C., Reitzel-Jaffe, D., & Lefebvre, L. (1995). *Factors associated with increased risk of gender-based violence among adolescents* (Manuscript under review). Ontario: University of Western Ontario, Department of Psychology.

Wolfe, D. A., Wekerle, C., & Scott, K. (in press). *Alternatives to violence: Empowering youth to promote healthy relationships*. Thousand Oaks, CA: Sage.

Resources

Printed Material

Carr, R., & Saunders, G. (1981). *Peer counseling starter kit.* Available from Peer Systems Consulting Group, Inc., 1052 Davie St., Victoria, BC V8S 4E3.

Date sexual assault (pamphlet). Available from the Sexual Assault Center, 700 Richmond Street, Suite 210, London, Ontario N6A 5C7.

Sexual assault: Dispelling the myths. Available from the Ontario Women's Directorate, 2 Carlton St., 12th floor, Toronto, Ontario M5B 2M9. (416) 597-4500

Wife assault: Dispelling the myths. Available from the Ontario Women's Directorate, 2 Carlton St., 12th floor, Toronto, Ontario M5B 2M9. (416) 597-4500

Videos

The following video is distributed by the National Film Board of Canada (Ottawa):

Crown prince. (1989). Produced by Joe MacDonald, directed by Aaron Kim Johnston; written by Don Bailey and Aaron Kim Johnston. Montreal: National Film Board of Canada.

The following videos are distributed by Kinetics Inc., 408 Dundas St. East, Toronto, Canada M5A 2A5. Phone: (416) 963-5979, Fax (416) 925-0653

1. *Date rape.* (1989). Produced by Patricia Depew; directed by Jesus S. Trevino; written by Bruce Harmon and Donald MacDonald.
2. *Dreamworlds: Desire/sex/power in rock video.* (1990). Written, edited, and narrated by Sut Jhally.
3. *Power to choose.* (1988). Produced by the Agency for Instructional Television, U.S.A.
4. *Right from the start: Dating violence prevention for teens.* (1992). Written by Judith Blackwell and Hilary Jones-Farrow, directed by Hilary Jones-Farrow; executive producer Jannit Rabinovitch; produced by Friday Street Productions Ltd. for the Victoria Women's Transition House Society, Victoria, B.C.

The following video is distributed by Esprit Films, 2 Lake Street, St. Catherine's, Ontario, (416) 685-8336:

1. *Break the cycle.* (1987). Produced and directed by Debbie Cartmer; Esprit Films.

About the Authors

David A. Wolfe (Principal Investigator) is Professor of Psychology and Psychiatry at the University of Western Ontario in London, Canada, and a founding member of the Center for Research on Violence Against Women and Children in London. As the former Director of Research for the Institute for the Prevention of Child Abuse in Toronto, he became involved in the development of policy and research aimed at the prevention of violence, which led to the beginnings of the Youth Relationships Project. His books include *Children of Battered Women* (with P. Jaffe and S. Wilson; Sage, 1990), *Child Abuse: Implications for Child Development and Psychopathology* (Sage, 1987), *Preventing Physical and Emotional Abuse of Children* (Guilford, 1991), and *Alternatives to Violence: Empowering Youth to Promote Healthy Relationships* (with C. Wekerle and K. Scott; Sage, in press).

Christine Wekerle (Co-Investigator) is Assistant Professor of Psychology at York University and has been involved with the YRP for several years during her doctoral work at the University of Western Ontario. Her research interests range across areas related to children and families (e.g., parenting problems, child abuse, and child maladjustment). She has published articles and chapters pertaining to the link between child maltreatment and adolescent outcomes, and she is coauthor (with D. Wolfe and K. Scott) of the forthcoming book, *Alternatives to Violence: Empowering Youth to Promote Healthy Relationships* (Sage, in press).

Robert Gough (Project Manager, 1992-1994) received his B.A. in Sociology from the University of Western Ontario in 1983. He was instrumental in designing the program format and curriculum for the YRP. Throughout his career, he has been involved in antiviolence work, specifically in the area of violence against women. He was the founding Director of Changing Ways (London) Inc., the program for abusive men in London, Ontario, Canada, and he has also presented at many conferences, professional development training sessions, public forums, and speaking engagements on the issue of men's violence. He is a past Chairperson of the London Coordinating Committee to End Woman Abuse, was a participant on a Woman Abuse Advisory Committee at the Ontario Police College, and has worked to establish a protocol in woman abuse cases with Correctional Services Canada. He was the recipient of the 1992 John Robinson Award for contributions toward ending violence against women. He is currently the Residence Program Coordinator at the University of Western Ontario.

Deborah Reitzel-Jaffe (Program Facilitator) is currently finishing her doctorate in clinical psychology at the University of Western Ontario, where she is focusing on the causes of relationship violence. She has published several journal articles and chapters on the topic of woman abuse and teen violence and has worked as a youth counselor and as cofacilitator of groups for youth that address violence in relationships.

Carolyn Grasley (Program Facilitator) is currently working on her doctorate in clinical psychology at the University of Western Ontario. Her master's degree and doctoral work reflect her special interest in the long-term repercussions of child sexual abuse for the development of adult intimate relationships. She has worked on the project as a research assistant and group facilitator.

Anna-Lee Pittman (Project Manager) received an M.L.I.S. from the University of Western Ontario in 1993. She is responsible for coordinating the research involved in this project and establishing the group program in local communities.

Lorraine Lefebvre (Research Assistant) received her B.A. from the University of Western Ontario in 1979 and has been involved in several clinical psychology projects over the past 14 years. She has worked since 1987 on projects dealing with the prevention of child sexual abuse and family violence and, most recently, the prevention of violence in adolescent relationships.

Jennifer Stumpf (Research Assistant) received her B.A. from McMaster University, Hamilton, Ontario. She is responsible for data collection from adolescents involved in the research aspect of this program.